The Time of Your Life

William Saroyan

B L O O M S B U R Y

LONDON · NEW DELHI · NEW YORK · SYDNEY

Bloomsbury Methuen Drama
An imprint of Bloomsbury Publishing Plc

50 Bedford Square	1385 Broadway
London	New York
WC1B 3DP	NY 10018
UK	USA

www.bloomsbury.com

Bloomsbury is a registered trade mark of Bloomsbury Publishing Plc

First published in the United Kingdom in 1983 by Methuen Drama
This edition published by Methuen Drama in 2008
Reprinted 2009, 2010, 2011, 2013

British Library Cataloguing-in-Publication Data
A catalogue record for this book is available from the British Library.

ISBN: PB: 978-1-4081-1394-3
EPDF: 978-1-4081-4116-8
EPUB: 978-1-4081-4117-5

Library of Congress Cataloging-in-Publication Data
A catalog record for this book is available from the Library of Congress.

Typeset by Country Setting, Kingsdown, Kent

The Time of Your Life
by William Saroyan

First performance at the Finborough Theatre, London
Wednesday, 26 November 2008

The Time of Your Life

by William Saroyan

Cast

Joe	**Alistair Cumming**
Tom	**Matthew Rowland Roberts**
Kitty Duval	**Maeve Malley-Ryan**
Nick	
Arab	
Kit Carson	**Robin Dunn**
McCarthy	**Jack Baldwin**
Krupp	**John Eastman**
Harry	**Omar Ibrahim**
Wesley	
Dudley	**Giles Roberts**
Elsie	**Natalie Britton**
Lorene	**Anne Bird**
Mary L	**Emma Vane**
Willie	**Kevin Millington**
Blick	**Gwilym Lloyd**
Ma	**Anne Bird**
A Society Gentleman	**Alex Dee**
A Society Lady	**Annie Julian**
Killer	**Larissa Archer**
Her Sidekick	**Nicola Sangster**
A Sailor	**David Palliser**
The Drunkard	**PJ King**
Cop	**Andy Root**
The Newsboy	**Anthony Kinahan**
Another Cop	**Hannah Scott**
Anna	**Olivia Missenden** or **Tanya Cooke**

Director	**Max Lewendel**
Designer	**Christopher Hone**
Lighting Designer	**Matthew Newbury**
Lighting Assistant	**Laurence Lindsay**
Sound Designer	**Joseph Thorpe**
Costume Designer	**Natasha Ward**
Costume Assistant	**Hannah Gibbs**
Assistant Directors	**Beth Pitts** and **Elizabeth Elstub**
Producers	**Aaron Prior** and **Tessa Sowry**
Associate Producer	**John Paul Micallef**
Stage Manager	**Bekah Wachenfeld**
Deputy Stage Manager	**Caroline Saunders**
Production Photography	**Arno**
Graphic Design	**Harry Osborne**

A bar in San Francisco, October 1939

There will be one interval of fifteen minutes.

The performance lasts approximately 2 hours and 30 minutes.

Our patrons are respectfully reminded that, in this intimate theatre, any noise such as rustling programmes, talking or the ringing of mobile phones may distract the actors and your fellow audience-members.

Interval drinks may be ordered in advance from the bar.

Works of William Saroyan used with permission of Stanford University.

William Saroyan Playwright
William Saroyan was born on 31 August 1908 in Fresno, California, to Armenian immigrant parents. In 1933, The Armenian journal Hairenik published William's first poetry and stories. In October of that year, he wrote his short-story masterpiece, The Daring Young Man on the Flying Trapeze. In 1939, Saroyan's first play, My Heart's in the Highlands, opened as a Group Theatre workshop production, to enthusiastic reviews. That summer, he wrote The Time of Your Life in a six-day stint. It was produced on Broadway by the Theatre Guild in 1939 with Joe Dowling, Celeste Holm and Gene Kelly, and won both the New York Critics Circle Award and the Pulitzer Prize. It has been revived three times on Broadway; was filmed in 1948, starring James Cagney; and twice filmed for TV including a PBS production in 1976 with Patti LuPone and Kevin Kline. It was last seen in the UK in a star-studded Royal Shakespeare Company production in Stratford and London in 1983, with John Thaw, Daniel Massey, Zoe Wanamaker, Miles Anderson, and Henry Goodman. William Saroyan died in Fresno, California, on May 18 1981. By his request, half of his ashes are interned in Fresno, the other half in Armenia.

Alistair Cumming Joe
Theatre includes The Queen of Spades and I (New End Theatre) and The Taming of the Shrew (Royal Shakespeare Company). Film includes Jerusalem, directed by Sam Taylor Wood, Niles, The Wolves of Kromer, Velvet Goldmine, Good Vibrations, The Hurting, Beyond Bedlam and Merlin. TV includes Skins, Tell Me, Rough Justice and Casualty. Radio includes Saint Nick.

Matthew Rowland-Roberts Tom
At the Finborough Theatre, Matthew has appeared in The Possibilities and Alfie. Trained at Middlesex University, University of South Florida and Guildford School of Acting. Theatre includes Oh! What A Lovely War (Buxton Opera House and National Tour), Steven Berkoff's Oedipus (Blackeyed Theatre Company), An Ideal Husband (Lyric Theatre), The Arabian Nights (Shakespeare's Globe), Titus Andronicus (National Tour), Much Ado About Nothing (Holland Park Theatre), Romeo and Juliet (Beirut), Twelfth Night (Bath Theatre Royal), Richard III (Swan Theatre, High Wycombe), Waiting for Lefty (BAC), Lorenzaccio (Young Vic) and Less (King's Head Theatre). TV includes Home and Away, Crimewatch UK, When Sex Goes Wrong and Morris 2274. Film includes Stephen Fry's Bright Young Things and Mirror, Mirror.

Maeve Malley-Ryan Kitty Duval
Trained at The Arts Educational Schools London. Theatre includes Dance Hall Days (Riverside Studios) and Under Which Flag? (Irish Repertory Theatre UK). TV includes Lewis. Film includes 28 Weeks Later. Radio includes The Family Project and The Language of Shadows.

Robin Dunn Kit Carson
Theatre includes work with Unity Theatre, Twelfth Night (Théâtre de Verdure, Paris), The Railway Children (National Tour), Death and Devil, The Madonna of St John's Wood and Thanatos (King's Head Theatre), Cock-A-Doodle Dandy and Uncle, Uncle (Baron's Court Theatre), Death of a Salesman, Dracula, The Playboy of the Western World and Taking Steps (Bridewell Theatre), and A Most Curious Murder - The Madeleine Smith Story (Edinburgh Festival). Film includes Richard Eyre's Stage Beauty.

Jack Baldwin McCarthy
Trained at the London Academy of Music and Dramatic Art. Theatre includes Party Time and Magnificence (Edinburgh Festival), Uncle Vanya, Henry IV Part I, Don Juan, What the Butler Saw, To the Green Fields Beyond and Mixed Up North, directed by Max Stafford-Clark (LAMDA), Antigone in the original Greek, The Hothouse, Stags and Hens, The Woman's Prize and The Caucasian Chalk Circle (KCL).

John Eastman Krupp
An associate member of the Icarus Theatre Collective, John appeared in their production of The Lesson (Old Red Lion Theatre, Edinburgh Festival, National Tour and winner of the Special Jury Prize at the Romanian Comedy Festival). Other Theatre includes Night, A Wall, Two Men (Brighton Festival) and Terminus (Jacaranda Theatre at RADA). TV in Australia includes Home and Away and Police Rescue.

Omar Ibrahim Harry
Trained at Guildford School of Acting where he played roles in Serious Money, Suburbia, The Kitchen, A Christmas Carol and A Comedy of Errors. This is Omar's professional debut. Writing includes a play, I Have A Penis.

Giles Roberts Dudley
Trained at The Oxford School of Drama. Theatre includes The Master and Margarita (The Space), The Revenger's Tragedy (Bridewell Theatre), Suburbia (Southwark Playhouse), Bingo (Theatre Royal Haymarket) and The Custom of the Country (White Bear Theatre). TV includes Operation Paraquat. Film includes The Boat That Rocked.

Natalie Britton Elsie
Trained at the Academy of Live and Recorded Arts. Theatre includes Twelfth Night (The Space), Small Craft Warnings (Landor Theatre), Unidentified Baggage (Henley Fringe Festival), Translations (The Producers Club, Off Broadway), Women of Troy, Cloudstreet and Comic Potential (ALRA). TV includes Lost in Austen.

Anne Bird Lorene / Ma
Theatre includes Gertrude's Secret (National Tour including the New End Theatre, Hampstead; Minerva Theatre, Chichester; Leeds Grand Theatre and the Oxford Playhouse; The Butterfly of Killybegs (Lyric Theatre, Belfast, and National Tour), Misery (Lyric Theatre, Belfast, and National Tour), Freefalling (Ardhowen Theatre, Enniskillen), The Playboy of the Western World (Liverpool Playhouse and Sheffield Crucible), Lazarus Man (Soho Theatre), Baby With the Bathwater (Old Red Lion Theatre) and The Vagina Monologues (Gate Theatre, London). TV includes Silent Witness and Lump. Radio includes The Unpredicted and Doctor Who – The Rapture.

Emma Vane Mary L
Trained at the Central School of Speech and Drama, and Drama Studio London. Theatre includes Playhouse Creatures (Theatre Royal Haymarket Apprenticeship Scheme 2008), A Great Undertaking in Little America (Alma Tavern, Bristol, and the White Bear Theatre) and Macbeth, The Comedy of Errors, Romeo and Juliet, and Exit the King. Film includes Fathers of Girls. Voiceovers include working as female station voice for Capital Radio London, GCAP Media's The One Network and London's Heart 106.2.

Kevin Millington Willie

Trained at the London Academy of Music and Dramatic Art. Theatre includes Thyestes (BAC), Taking Sides (Linbury Studio Theatre, Royal Opera House), Richard II and Henry IV (MacOwan Theatre) and Much Ado About Nothing (Old Sorting Office, Barnes), Your Ex-Lover is Dead (The Arches, Glasgow), Canada Day, 1995 (Forest Fringe Theatre) and Strippers and Gentlemen (Edinburgh Festival). TV includes The Shooting Party and Modern City Mimicry. Film includes Joe's A Wanker and the forthcoming Vuelve a Mi.

Gwilym Lloyd Blick

Trained at Drama Centre London and Vahktangov Institute Moscow. Theatre includes The Provoked Wife and A Winters Tale (Courtyard Theatre), Wired (King's Head Theatre), Black Light and After Everything (Union Theatre), The Bear (Lion and Unicorn Theatre), Bacchaeful (Area 10 Project Space), Measure for Measure Rosemary Branch Theatre), Two Gentlemen of Verona and Five Kinds of Silence (Drak Edge Theatre), and As You Like It (Shakespeare's Globe).

Alex Dee A Society Gentleman

Theatre includes Equus, Metamorphosis, Farewell Miss Julie Logan, Return to the Forbidden Planet, Spite the Face (Edinburgh Festival). Film includes The Wind That Shakes the Barley. TV includes the BAFTA winning Spooks Interactive.

Annie Julian A Society Lady

At the Finborough Theatre, Annie appeared in Coyote Ugly for the Icarus Theatre Collective. Trained at Drama Studio London. Theatre includes The Waves (The Drill Hall), Bluebeard, The Arc, The Bride and the Coffin and Be My Baby and Snapshot (Old Red Lion Theatre), Fatale (Bridewell Theatre), Twelfth Night (Courtyard Theatre), The Railway Children (King's Head Theatre), The Play (Barons Court Theatre), Still Life (Taplow Festival), Time and the Conways (Theatre 503), and the spoken/art exhibit ReLocate: The Stephen Lawrence Murder. TV includes EastEnders, Doctors, Canterbury Tales: The Wife of Bath's Tale, Saxondale, Mad About Alice, and NCS:Manhunt .

Larissa Archer Killer

At the Finborough Theatre, Larissa appeared in the New Work America season in a reading of Mr Marmalade. Trained at the Central School of Speech and Drama. Theatre includes Fetes de la Unit (Berkeley Repertory Theater), Icarus's Mother and Boy's Life (Actors Theatre of San Francisco), Popping the Cherry (Actors Theatre of San Francisco and New York), Sister Mary Ignatius Explains it All for You (Shelton Theatre), The Glory of Living (San Francisco Playhouse), and The Broken Heart and The Tempest (Embassy Theatre).

Nicola Sangster Her Sidekick

Trained at the Birmingham School of Speech and Drama. Theatre includes Much Ado About Nothing (Clockhouse Theatre, Guernsey), Tales from Ovid (Birmingham Old Rep), Female Transport (Birmingham Library Theatre), Charlotte's Web (National Tour) and Laura's Star (National Tour and I Theatre, Singapore). Recordings include the unabridged audiobook of Fanny Hill.

David Palliser Sailor

Trained at LAMDA. Productions in training include The Cherry Orchard, Titus Andronicus, King Henry IV Part One and The Man of Mode (Linbury Studio Theatre, Royal Opera House), and Journey's End, The Caucasian Chalk Circle, Pericles and Can-Can (MacOwan Theatre). Theatre includes The Late Mattia Pascal (Bolona, Italy), Arcadia and Company (SLOCA, Melbourne), and Medea and Alcestis (Melbourne). Film includes Corkscrewed.

PJ King The Drunkard
Trained at the London Academy of Performing Arts. Theatre includes Dinner (Upstairs at the Gatehouse), Sleuth (Greenwich Theatre), Art (Stage Door Theatre, Florida), Mothers Gift and Black Comedy (Waterfront Playhouse, Florida), Orson's Shadow (Miami Lakes Theatre, Florida), On Golden Pond and Other Peoples Money (Public Theatre of South Florida), Sherlock's Secret Life (Red Barn Theatre, Key West) and Reality TV (Edge Theatre, Florida). TV includes Crop Circles and The Days That Shook the World. Film includes Photo Shoot and Quiet Storm.

Andy Root Cop
Trained at the Royal Scottish Academy of Music and Drama. Theatre includes Much Ado About Nothing (Bard in the Botanics, Glasgow), The Merchant of Venice (Bard in the Botanics, Glasgow) and Peter Pan (Citizens Theatre, Glasgow).

Anthony Kinahan The Newsboy
Trained at the Central School of Speech and Drama. Theatre includes roles in Romeo and Juliet (Dundalk Town Hall), Hamlet (The Hub, Dublin), Follies and Ragtime (O'Reilly Theatre, Dublin), Shaw in Lust (Filmbase, Dublin), Love's Labour's Lost and Old Bachelor (Tallaght Theatre, Dublin), The Devil's Tale and Mathilde (Embassy Theatre) and Me and My Girl (London Palladium).

Hannah Scott Another Cop
Hannah trained at the Central School of Speech and Drama. Theatre includes Barbarians (Salisbury Playhouse), Aladdin (Theatr Clwyd), Into The Woods (New Oxford Theatre), Silvercube (Soho Theatre Studio), Low Dat (Hampstead Theatre), A Midsummer Night's Dream (Open Air Tour), Sweeney Todd (Embassy Theatre) and Me and My Girl (London Palladium). Film includes Semi-Skimmed, When Yesterday is Tomorrow, and Deep River Rock.

Olivia Missenden Anna
Training at the Italia Conti Academy of Theatre Arts. Theatre includes a rehearsed reading of Denied (Theatre Royal Haymarket) and Beauty and the Beast (Spillers Productions). TV includes Lady Killers and a commercial for Grand Designs. Corporate work includes playing Lucy in the Narnia DVD launch of The Lion, the Witch and the Wardrobe.

Tanya Cooke Anna
Training at the Italia Conti Academy of Theatre Arts. As well as many in house productions including Legends (performed at New Wimbledon Theatre), she was a vocalist for Mamma Mia the Movie (recorded with HotHouse Music).

Max Lewendel Director
At the Finborough Theatre, Max has directed James Graham's Albert's Boy, starring Tony award-winner Victor Spinetti, and the Time Out Critics' Choice production of Coyote Ugly; and also co-produced the UK premiere of Frank McGuinness' Gates of Gold. Trained at the Illinois Wesleyan School of Drama in Bloomington, Illinois, Max founded the Icarus Theatre Collective in 2004. Last year, Max directed an international tour of Ionesco's The Lesson which transferred to the Assembly Rooms, Edinburgh, Old Red Lion Theatre, and Romania, winning rave reviews and two major awards. He also co-directed Engage's production of Lost Children (Tour of East Anglia, Holland and Kenya). In 2009, he will be directing two mid-scale tours: Othello and Nicholas Wright's Vincent in Brixton. www.icarustheatre.co.uk

Christopher Hone Designer
At the Finborough Theatre, he designed Coyote Ugly for the Icarus Theatre Collective and Italian-American Reconciliation. Trained in Theatre Design at Nottingham Trent University. Theatre includes One Minute (Courtyard Theatre), Guerrilla/Whore (Tabard

Theatre), Here (Tristan Bates Theatre), The Lesson (Icarus Theatre Collective), Meta
morphosis (Brockley Jack), A Doll's House (New Wimbledon Studio), Equus (Waverley
Studio, Nottingham) and Italian American Reconciliation (South East tour). TV and Film
includes Big Brother 7, Celebrity Big Brother 4 and 5, The Disappeared, a commercial
for the novel Small World, and for QVC.

Matthew Newbury Lighting
Lighting Designs include Icarus Theatre Collective's The Lesson (Old Red Lion Theatre,
International Tour and Teatrul de Comedie, Bucharest), Chicken Soup with Barley
(Tricycle Theatre), The Graduate (Tallahassee, Florida), Terrorism and Bluebirds
(Cochrane Theatre), Parade (The Hub, Haywards Heath), Metamorphosis (Capitol
Theatre, Horsham, and National Tour), Picnic at Hanging Rock (Minerva Theatre,
Chichester), Bat Boy, Confusions, The Sea and Nicholas Nickleby (Guildford School
of Acting), Mary Kelly's Bed, The Gilded Lilies and Walk in the Shadow (Watermill
Theatre, Newbury) and The Mikado (York Theatre Royal). Matthew also works as an
assistant to Richard G. Jones including SpongeBob Squarepants Live (Kuala Lumpur,
Singapore, and Asian Tour), Sweeney Todd (New Ambassadors Theatre, National
Tour and Watermill Theatre), Mack and Mabel (Criterion Theatre, National Tour and
Watermill Theatre), Steptoe and Son (Comedy Theatre), Flower Girls (Hampstead
Theatre), Horrid Henry (Lyceum Theatre, Sheffield, and National Tour) and All Quiet on
the Western Front (Nottingham Playhouse and National Tour).

Joseph Thorpe Sound Designer
Trained at Rose Bruford College. Sound Designs include Dry Lighting (King's Head
Theatre), Subject to Change and Bare Bones (Birds Nest, Deptford) and Rough Curves
(Southwark Playhouse Café). He is Resident Sound Designer for The Lab Theatre
Collective at The Birds Nest, Deptford. He also works as a Sound Technician and
Engineer including recordings for Lotus Pedals for Forkbeard Fantasy's production of
Invisible Bonfires.

Natasha Ward Costume Designer
Trained at the Central School of Speech and Drama in Set and Costume Design.
Designs include Rue Magique (King's Head Theatre), Henry V (National Tour for Love
and Madness), Carrie's War (Lilian Baylis Theatre), Something in Common (Claque
Theatre, Seven Streams Community), and The Living Unknown Soldier (Arcola
Theatre). She was Wardrobe Mistress for three UK National Tours – Martha, Josie
and the Chinese Elvis (Birmingham Rep), Terms of Endearment (York Theatre Royal)
and The Clean House (Royal and Derngate Theatre, Northampton). Films include Mr
Perfect.

Beth Pitts Assistant Director
Bethany studied English, Writing and Performance at York Univerisity. She has since
worked as a Production Assistant for Whippet Productions, stage managing Natural
Selection (Theatre 503) and Many Roads to Paradise (Finborough Theatre).

Elizabeth Elstub Assistant Director
This is Elizabeth's debut as an assistant director. As an actress, she has appeared
in Ghosts (Barons Court Theatre), 'Tis Pity She's a Whore (Jermyn Street Theatre),
Uncle Vanya (Union Theatre) and Massa (Camden's Peoples Theatre). Film includes 28
Weeks Later and Sweeney Todd.

Aaron Prior Producer
At the Finborough Theatre, Aaron produced the world premiere of When Midnight
Strikes. Aaron has worked extensively as a producer, performer and stage manager.
He is currently the Resident Company Stage Manager of the Musical Theatre Academy,
a performance based teaching company in Telford, Shropshire. Aaron also operates
his own production company and corporate entertainment provider, Work The Room

Entertainments Ltd. www.worktherooments.co.uk

Tessa Sowry Producer
Trained at Brunel University. Since graduating, she has worked briefly for numerous companies including Arts Council England, Julie McNamara and the Gate Theatre. This is her producing debut.

John Paul Micallef Associate Producer
John Paul is a producer working in theatre, film and TV. He is presently developing a TV series Last Breath for a major US network, and is in pre-production for a feature film, Alone, due to commence shooting in Malta in Summer 2009. John Paul is active in commissioning new writers, both in theatre and film, and one of these projects, Coward, is due to open in a central London theatre in Spring 2009.

Bekah Wachenfeld Stage Manager
At the Finborough Theatre, Bekah has been Assistant Stage Manager for Cradle Me and Follow. Trained at James Madison University in Harrisonburg, Virginia. Stage management includes The Real Inspector Hound, Jane Eyre and Twelfth Night (James Madison University), and Doubt, The Light in the Piazza and Les Miserables (Weston Playhouse, Vermont). She was nominated for the Kennedy Center American College Theatre Festival Stage Management Fellowship.

Acknowledgements
Pommery Champagne
All Nations Church, Clapham Park
The Stag Pub, Victoria
The Club for Acts and Actors
Helen Ross

The Time of Your Life was first presented at the Shubert Theatre, New Haven, USA, on 7 October 1939. It was directed by Eddie Dowling and William Saroyan, and transferred first to Boston and then to the Booth Theatre in New York. It was awarded the Pulitzer Prize and the Drama Critics' Award.

The Time of Your Life

In the time of your life, live – so that in that good time there shall be no ugliness or death for yourself or for any life your life touches. Seek goodness everywhere, and when it is found, bring it out of its hiding place and let it be free and unashamed. Place in matter and in flesh the least of the values, for these are the things that hold death and must pass away. Discover in all things that which shines and is beyond corruption. Encourage virtue in whatever heart it may have been driven into secrecy and sorrow by the shame and terror of the world. Ignore the obvious, for it is unworthy of the clear eye and the kindly heart. Be the inferior of no man, nor of any man be the superior. Remember that every man is a variation of yourself. No man's guilt is not yours, nor is any man's innocence a thing apart. Despise evil and ungodliness, but not men of ungodliness or evil. These, understand. Have no shame in being kindly and gentle, but if the time comes in the time of your life to kill, kill and have no regret. In the time of your life, live – so that in the wondrous time you shall not add to the misery and sorrow of the world, but shall smile to the infinite delight and mystery of it.

The Place

Nick's Pacific Street Saloon, Restaurant and Entertainment Palace at the foot of Embarcadero, in San Francisco. A suggestion of Room 21 at the New York Hotel, upstairs, around the corner.

The Time

Afternoon and night of a day in October 1939.

The People

Joe, *a young loafer with money and a good heart*

Tom, *his admirer, disciple, errand boy, stooge and friend*

Kitty Duval, *a young woman, with memories*

Nick, *owner of Nick's Pacific Street Saloon, Restaurant and Entertainment Palace*

Arab, *an Eastern philosopher and harmonica player*

Kit Carson, *an old Indian-fighter*

McCarthy, *an intelligent and well-read longshoreman*

Krupp, *his boyhood friend, a waterfront cop who hates his job but doesn't know what else to do instead*

Harry, *a natural-born hoofer who wants to make people laugh but can't*

Wesley, *a coloured boy who plays a mean and melancholy boogie-woogie piano*

Dudley, *a young man in love*

Elsie, *a nurse, the girl he loves*

Lorene, *an unattractive woman*

Mary L, *an unhappy woman of quality and great beauty*

Willie, *a marble-game maniac*

Blick, *a heel*

A Sailor

Ma, *Nick's mother*

A Society Gentleman

A Society Lady

Killer, *a streetwalker*

Her **Sidekick**

The Drunkard

A Cop

The Newsboy

Another Cop

Anna, *Nick's daughter*

Act One

Nick's is an American place; a San Francisco waterfront honky-tonk.

At a table, **Joe***: always calm, always quiet, always thinking, always eager, always bored, always superior. His expensive clothes are casually and youthfully worn and give him an almost boyish appearance. He is thinking.*

Behind the bar, **Nick***: a big red-headed young Italian-American with an enormous naked woman tattooed in red on the inside of his right arm. He is studying the* Racing *Form.*

The **Arab**, *at his place at the end of the bar. He is a lean old man with a rather ferocious old-country moustache, with the ends twisted up. Between the thumb and forefinger of his left hand is the Mohammedan tattoo indicating that he has been to Mecca. He is sipping a glass of beer.*

It is about eleven thirty in the morning.

Sam *is sweeping out. We see only his back. He disappears into the kitchen. The* **Sailor** *at the bar finishes his drink and leaves, moving thoughtfully, as though he were trying very hard to discover how to live.*

The **Newsboy** *comes in.*

Newsboy (*cheerfully*)   Good morning, everybody. (*No answer. To* **Nick**.) Paper, Mister?

Nick *shakes his head, no. The* **Newsboy** *goes to* **Joe**.

Newsboy   Paper, Mister?

Joe *shakes his head, no. The* **Newsboy** *walks away, counting papers.*

Joe (*noticing him*)   How many you got?

Newsboy   Five.

Joe *gives him a quarter, takes all the papers, glances at the headlines with irritation, throws them away. The* **Newsboy** *watches carefully, then goes.*

Arab (*picks up paper, looks at headlines, shakes head as if rejecting everything else a man might say about the world*)   No foundation. All the way down the line.

The **Drunkard** *comes in. Walks to the telephone, looks for a nickel in the chute, sits down at* **Joe***'s table.* **Nick** *takes the* **Drunkard** *out. The* **Drunkard** *returns.*

Drunkard (*champion of the Bill of Rights*)   This is a free country, ain't it?

Willie*, the marble-game maniac, explodes through the swinging doors and lifts the forefinger of his right hand comically, indicating one beer. He is a very young man, not more than twenty. He is wearing heavy shoes, a pair of old and dirty corduroys, a little green turtleneck jersey with a large letter 'F' on the chest, an oversize two-button tweed coat, and a green hat, with the brim up.* **Nick** *sets out a glass of beer for him, he drinks it, straightens up vigorously, saying 'Aaah', makes a solemn face, gives* **Nick** *a one-finger salute of adieu, and begins to leave, refreshed and restored in spirit. He walks by the marble game, halts suddenly, turns, studies the contraption, gestures as if to say, 'Oh, no.' Turns to go, stops, returns to the machine, studies it, takes a handful of small coins out of his pants' pocket, lifts a nickel, indicates with a gesture, 'One game, no more.' Puts the nickel in the slot, pushes in the slide, making an interesting noise.*

Nick   You can't beat that machine.

Willie   Oh yeah?

The marbles fall, roll, and take their place. He pushes down the lever, placing one marble in position. Takes a very deep breath, walks in a small circle, excited at the beginning of great drama. Stands straight and pious before the contest. Himself versus the cunning and trickery of the novelty industry of America, and the whole challenging world. He is the last of the American pioneers, with nothing more to fight but the machine, with no other reward than lights going on and off, and six nickels for one. Before him is the last champion, the machine. He is the last challenger, the young man with nothing to do in the world. **Willie** *grips the knob delicately, studies the situation carefully, draws the knob back, holds it a moment and then releases it. The first marble rolls out among the hazards, and the contest is on. At the very beginning of the play 'The Missouri Waltz' is coming from the phonograph. The music ends here. This is the signal for the beginning of the play.* **Joe** *suddenly comes out of his reverie. He whistles the way people do who are calling a cab that's about a block* *away, only he does it quietly.* **Willie** *turns around, but* **Joe** *gestures for him to return to his work.* **Nick** *looks up from the* Racing Form.

Joe (*calling*)   Tom. (*To himself.*) Where the hell is he, every time I need him?

He looks around calmly: the nickel-in-the-slot phonograph in the corner; the open public telephone; the stage; the marble game; the bar; and so on. He calls again, this time very loud.

Hey, Tom.

Nick (*with morning irritation*)   What do you want?

Joe (*without thinking*)   I want the boy to get me a watermelon, that's what *I* want. What do *you* want? Money, or love, or fame, or what? You won't get them studying the *Racing Form.*

Nick   I like to keep abreast of the times.

Tom *comes hurrying in. He is a great big man of about thirty or so who appears to be much younger because of the childlike expression of his face; handsome, dumb, innocent, troubled, and a little bewildered by everything. He is obviously adult in years, but it seems as if by all rights he should still be a boy. He is defensive as clumsy, self-conscious, overgrown boys are. He is wearing a flashy cheap suit.* **Joe** *leans back and studies him with casual disapproval.* **Tom** *slackens his pace and becomes clumsy and embarrassed, waiting for the bawling-out he's pretty sure he's going to get.*

Joe (*objectively, severely, but a little amused*)   Who saved your life?

Tom (*sincerely*)   You did, Joe. Thanks.

Joe (*interested*)   How'd I do it?

Tom (*confused*)   What?

Joe (*even more interested*)   *How'd I do it?*

Tom   Joe, you know how you did it.

Joe (*softly*)   I want you to answer me. How'd I save your life? I've forgotten.

Tom (*remembering, with a big sorrowful smile*)   You made me eat all that chicken soup three years ago when I was sick and hungry.

Joe (*fascinated*)   *Chicken soup?*

Tom (*eagerly*)   Yeah.

Joe   Three years? Is it that long?

Tom (*delighted to have the information*)   Yeah, sure. 1937. 1938. 1939. This is 1939, Joe.

Joe (*amused*)   Never mind what year it is. Tell me the whole story.

Tom   You took me to the doctor. You gave me money for food and clothes, and paid my room rent. Aw, Joe, you know all the different things you did.

Joe *nods, turning away from* **Tom** *after each question.*

Joe   You in good health now?

Tom   Yeah, Joe.

Joe   You got clothes?

Tom   Yeah, Joe.

Joe   You eat three times a day. Sometimes four?

Tom   Yeah, Joe. Sometimes five.

Joe   You got a place to sleep?

Tom   Yeah, Joe.

Joe *nods. Pauses. Studies* **Tom** *carefully.*

Joe   Then, where the hell have you been?

Tom (*humbly*)   Joe, I was out in the street listening to the boys. They're talking about the trouble down here on the waterfront.

Joe (*sharply*)   I want you to be around when I need you.

Tom (*pleased that the bawling-out is over*)   I won't do it again. Joe, one guy out there says there's got to be a revolution before anything will ever be all right.

Joe (*impatient*)   I know all about it. Now, here. Take this money. Go up to the Emporium. You know where the Emporium is?

Tom   Yeah, sure, Joe.

Joe   All right. Take the elevator and go up to the fourth floor. Walk around to the back, to the toy department. Buy me a couple of dollars' worth of toys and bring them here.

Tom (*amazed*)   Toys? What *kind* of toys, Joe?

Joe   Any kind of toys. Little ones that I can put on this table.

Tom   What do you want toys for, Joe?

Joe (*mildly angry*)   *What?*

Tom   All right, all right. You don't have to get sore at *everything*. What'll people think, a big guy like me buying toys?

Joe   *What people?*

Tom   Aw, Joe, you're always making me do crazy things for you, and *I'm* the guy that gets embarrassed. You just sit in this place and make me do all the dirty work.

Joe (*looking away*)   Do what I tell you.

Tom   OK, but I wish I knew *why*. (*He makes to go.*)

Joe   Wait a minute. Here's a nickel. Put it in the phonograph. Number seven. I want to hear that waltz again.

Tom   Boy, I'm glad I don't have to stay and listen to it. Joe, what do you hear in that song anyway? We listen to that song ten times a day. Why can't we hear number six, or two, or nine? There are a lot of other numbers.

Joe (*emphatically*)   Put the nickel in the phonograph. (*Pause.*) Sit down and wait till the music's over. Then go get me some toys.

Tom   OK. OK.

Joe (*loudly*)   Never mind being a martyr about it either. The cause isn't worth it.

Tom *puts the nickel into the machine, with a ritual of impatient and efficient movement which plainly shows his lack of sympathy or enthusiasm. His manner also reveals, however, that his lack of sympathy is spurious and exaggerated. Actually, he is fascinated by the music, but is so confused by it that he pretends he dislikes it.*

The music begins. It is another variation of 'The Missouri Waltz', played dreamily and softly, with perfect orchestral form, and with a theme of weeping in the horns repeated a number of times.

At first **Tom** *listens with something close to irritation, since he can't understand what is so attractive in the music to* **Joe**, *and what is so painful and confusing in it to himself. Very soon, however, he is carried away by the melancholy story of grief and nostalgia of the song.*

He stands, troubled by the poetry and confusion in himself.

Joe, *on the other hand, listens as if he were not listening, indifferent and unmoved. What he's interested in is* **Tom**. *He turns and glances at* **Tom**.

Kitty Duval, *who lives in a room in the New York Hotel, around the corner, comes beyond the swinging doors quietly, and walks slowly to the bar, her reality and rhythm a perfect accompaniment to the sorrowful American music, which is her music, as it is* **Tom**'s. *Which the world drove out of her, putting in its place brokenness and all manner of spiritually crippled forms. She seems to understand this, and is angry. Angry with herself, full of hate for the poor world, and full of pity and contempt for its tragic, unbelievable, confounded people. She is a small, powerful girl, with that kind of delicate and rugged beauty which no circumstance of evil or ugly reality can destroy. This beauty is that element of the immortal which is in the seed of good and common people, and which is kept alive in some of the female of our kind, no matter how accidentally or pointlessly they may have entered the world.* **Kitty Duval** *is somebody. There is an angry purity and a fierce pride in her.*

In her stance, and way of walking, there is grace and arrogance, **Joe** *recognises her as a great person immediately. She goes to the bar.*

Kitty   Beer.

Nick *places a glass of beer before her mechanically.*

She swallows half the drink, and listens to the music again.

Tom *turns and sees her. He becomes dead to everything in the world but her. He stands like a lump, fascinated and undone by his almost religious adoration for her.* **Joe** *notices* **Tom**.

Joe (*gently*)   Tom.

Tom *begins to move toward the bar, where* **Kitty** *is standing.*

Joe (*loudly*)   Tom.

Tom *halts, then turns, and* **Joe** *motions to him to come over to the table. He goes over.*

Joe (*quietly*)   Have you got everything straight?

Tom (*out of the world*)   What?

Joe   What do you mean, what? I just gave you some instructions.

Tom (*pathetically*)   What do you want, Joe?

Joe   I want you to come to your senses.

He stands up quietly and knocks **Tom**'s *hat off.* **Tom** *picks up his hat quickly.*

Tom   I got it, Joe. I got it. The Emporium. Fourth floor. In the back. The toy department. Two dollars' worth of toys. That you can put on a table.

Kitty (*to herself*)   Who the hell is he to push a big man like that around?

Joe   I'll expect you back in a half-hour. Don't get sidetracked anywhere. Just do what I tell you.

Tom (*pleading*)   Joe? Can't I bet four bits on a horse race? There's a long shot – Precious Time – that's going to win by ten lengths. I got to have money.

Joe *points to the street.* **Tom** *goes out.* **Nick** *is combing his hair, looking in the mirror.*

Nick   I thought you wanted him to get you a watermelon.

Joe   I forgot. (*He watches* **Kitty** *a moment. To* **Kitty**, *clearly, slowly, with great compassion.*) What's the dream?

Kitty (*moving to* **Joe**, *coming to*)   What?

Joe (*holding the dream for her*)   What's the dream, *now*?

Kitty (*coming still closer*)   What dream?

Joe   What dream! The dream you're dreaming.

Nick   Suppose he did bring you a watermelon? What the hell would you do with it?

Joe (*irritated*)   I'd put in on this table. I'd look at it. Then I'd eat it. What do you *think* I'd do with it, sell it for a profit?

Nick   How should I know what *you'd* do with *anything*? What I'd like to know is, where do you get your money from? What work do you do?

Joe (*looking at* **Kitty**)   Bring us a bottle of champagne.

Kitty   Champagne?

Joe (*simply*)   Would you rather have something else?

Kitty   What's the big idea?

Joe   I thought you might like some champagne. I myself am very fond of it.

Kitty   Yeah, but what's the big idea? You can't push *me* around.

Joe (*gently, but severely*)   It's not in my nature to be unkind to another human being. I have only contempt for wit. Otherwise I might say something obvious, therefore cruel, and perhaps untrue.

Kitty   You be careful what you think about me.

Joe (*slowly, not looking at her*)   I have only the noblest thoughts for both your person, and your spirit.

Nick (*having listened carefully and not being able to make it out*)   What are you talking about?

Kitty   You shut up. You –

Joe   He owns this place. He's an important man. All kinds of people come to him looking for work. Comedians. Singers. Dancers.

Kitty   I don't care. He can't call me names.

Nick   All right, sister. I know how it is with a two-dollar whore in the morning.

Kitty (*furiously*)   Don't you dare call me names. I used to be in burlesque.

Nick   If you were ever in burlesque, I used to be Charlie Chaplin.

Kitty (*angry and a little pathetic*)   I *was* in burlesque. I played the burlesque circuit from coast to coast. I've had flowers sent to me by European royalty. I've had dinner with young men of wealth and social position.

Nick   You're dreaming.

Kitty (*to* **Joe**)   *I was in burlesque.* Kitty Duval. That was my name. Life-size photographs of me in costume in front of burlesque theatres all over the country.

Joe (*gently, coaxingly*)   I believe you. Have some champagne.

Nick (*going to table, with champagne bottle and glasses*)   There he goes again.

Joe   Miss Duval?

Kitty (*sincerely, going over*)   That's not my *real* name. That's my *stage* name.

Joe   I'll call you by your stage name.

Nick (*pouring*)   All right, sister, make up your mind. Are you going to have champagne with him, or not?

Joe   Pour the lady some wine.

Nick   OK, Professor. Why you come to this joint instead of one of the high-class dumps uptown is more than I can understand. Why don't you have champagne at the St Francis? Why don't you drink with a lady?

Kitty (*furiously*)   Don't you call me names – you dentist.

Joe   Dentist?

Nick (*amazed, loudly*)   What kind of cussing is that? (*Pause. Looking at* **Kitty**, *then at* **Joe**, *bewildered.*) This guy doesn't belong here. The only reason I've got champagne is because *he* keeps ordering it all the time. (*To* **Kitty**.) Don't think you're the only one he drinks champagne with. He drinks with *all* of them. (*Pause.*) He's crazy. Or something.

Joe (*confidentially*)   Nick, I think you're going to be all right in a couple of centuries.

Nick   I'm sorry, I don't understand your English.

Joe *lifts his glass.* **Kitty** *slowly lifts hers, not quite sure of what's going on.*

Joe (*sincerely*)   To the spirit, Kitty Duval.

Kitty (*beginning to understand, and very grateful, looking at him*) Thank you.

They drink.

Joe (*calling*)   Nick.

Nick   Yeah?

Joe   Would you mind putting a nickel in the machine again? Number –

Nick   Seven. I know. I know. I don't mind at all, Your Highness, although, personally, I'm not a lover of music. (*Going to the machine.*) As a matter of fact I think Tchaikovsky was a dope.

Joe   Tchaikovsky? Where'd you ever hear of Tchaikovsky?

Nick   He was a dope.

Joe   Yeah. Why?

Nick   They talked about him on the radio one Sunday morning. He was a sucker. He let a woman drive him crazy.

Joe   I see.

Nick   I stood behind that bar listening to the goddamn stuff and cried like a baby. *None but the lonely heart!* He was a dope.

Joe   What made you cry?

Nick   What?

Joe (*sternly*)   What made you cry, Nick?

Nick (*angry with himself*)   I don't know.

Joe   I've been underestimating you, Nick. Play number seven.

Nick   They get everybody worked up. They give everybody stuff they shouldn't have.

He puts the nickel into the machine and the waltz begins again. He listens to the music. Then studies the Racing Form.

Kitty (*to herself, dreaming*)   I like champagne, and everything that goes with it. Big houses with big porches, and big rooms with big windows, and big lawns, and big trees, and flowers growing everywhere, and big shepherd dogs sleeping in the shade.

Nick   I'm going next door to Frankie's to make a bet. I'll be right back.

Joe   Make one for me.

Nick (*going to* **Joe**)   Who do you like?

Joe (*giving him the money*)   Precious Time.

Nick   *Ten dollars?* Across the board?

Joe   No. On the nose.

Nick   OK. (*He goes.*)

Dudley R. Bostwick, *as he calls himself, breaks through the swinging doors, and practically flings himself upon the open telephone beside the phonograph.*

Dudley *is a young man of about twenty-four or twenty-five, ordinary and yet extraordinary. He is smallish, as the saying is, neatly dressed in bargain clothes, overworked and irritated by the routine and dullness and monotony of his life, apparently nobody and nothing, but in reality a great personality. The swindled young man. Educated, but without the least real understanding. A brave, dumb, salmon-spirit struggling for life in weary,* *stupefied flesh, duelling ferociously with a banal mind which has been only irritated by what it has been taught. He is a great personality because, against all these handicaps, what he wants is simple and basic: a woman. This urgent and violent need, common yet miraculous enough in itself, considering the unhappy environment of the animal, is the force which elevates him from nothingness to greatness. A ridiculous greatness, but in the nature of things beautiful to behold.*

All that he has been taught, and everything he believes, is phoney, and yet he himself is real, almost super-real, because of this indestructible force in himself. His face is ridiculous. His personal rhythm is tense and jittery. His speech is shrill and violent. His gestures are wild. His ego is disjointed and epileptic. And yet deeply he possesses the same wholeness of spirit, and directness of energy, that is in all species of animals. There is little innate or cultivated spirit in him, but there is no absence of innocent animal force. He is a young man who has been taught that he has a chance, as a person, and believes it. As a matter of fact, he hasn't a chance in the world, and should have been told by somebody, or should not have had his natural and valuable ignorance spoiled by education, ruining an otherwise perfectly good and charming member of the human race.

At the telephone he immediately begins to dial furiously, hesitates, changes his mind, stops dialling, hangs up furiously, and suddenly begins again.

Not more than half a minute after the firecracker arrival of **Dudley R. Bostwick**, *occurs the polka-and-waltz arrival of* **Harry**.

Harry *is another story. He comes in timidly, turning about uncertainly, awkward, out of place everywhere, embarrassed and encumbered by the contemporary costume, sick at heart, but determined to fit in somewhere. His arrival constitutes a dance.*

His clothes don't fit. The pants are a little too large. The coat, which doesn't match, is also a little too large, and loose.

He is a dumb young fellow, but he has ideas. A philosophy, in fact. His philosophy is simple and beautiful. The world is sorrowful. The world needs laughter. **Harry** *is funny. The world needs* **Harry**. **Harry** *will make the world laugh.*

He has probably had a year or two of high school. He has also listened to the boys at the pool room.

He's looking for **Nick***. He goes to the* **Arab***, and says, 'Are you Nick?'*
The **Arab** *shakes his head. He stands at the bar, waiting. He waits very*
busily.

Harry (*as* **Nick** *returns*)   You Nick?

Nick (*very loudly*)   I am Nick.

Harry (*acting*)   Can you use a great comedian?

Nick (*behind the bar*)   Who, for instance?

Harry (*almost angry*)   Me.

Nick   You? What's funny about you?

Dudley*, at the telephone, is dialling. Because of some defect in the*
apparatus the dialling is very loud.

Dudley   Hello. Sunset 7349? May I speak to Miss Elsie
Mandelspiegel?

Pause.

Harry (*with spirit and noise, dancing*)   I dance and do gags and
stuff.

Nick   In costume? Or are you wearing your costume?

Dudley   All I need is a cigar.

Kitty (*continuing the dream of grace*)   I'd walk out of the house,
and stand on the porch, and look at the trees, and smell the
flowers, and run across the lawn, and lie down under a tree,
and read a book. (*Pause.*) A book of poems, maybe.

Dudley (*very, very clearly*)   Elsie Mandelspiegel. (*Impatiently.*) She
has a room on the fourth floor. She's a nurse at the Southern
Pacific Hospital. Elsie Mandelspiegel. She works at night. Elsie.
Yes.

He begins waiting again. **Wesley***, a coloured boy, comes to the bar and*
stands near **Harry***, waiting.*

Nick   Beer?

Wesley   No, sir. I'd like to talk to you.

Nick (*to* **Harry**)   All right. Get funny.

Harry (*getting funny, an altogether different person, an actor with great energy, both in power of voice, and in force and speed of physical gesture*) Now, I'm standing on the corner of Third and Market. I'm looking around. I'm figuring it out. There it is. Right in front of me. The whole city. The whole world. People going by. They're going somewhere. I don't know where, but they're going. I ain't going *anywhere*. Where the hell can you go? I'm figuring it out. All right. I'm a citizen. A fat guy bumps his stomach into the face of an old lady. They were in a hurry. Fat and old. *They bumped.* Boom. I don't know. It may mean war. *War.* Germany. England. Russia. I don't know for sure.

Loudly, dramatically, he salutes, about faces, presents arms, aims and fires.

WAAAAAR.

He blows a call to arms. **Nick** *gets sick of this, indicates with a gesture that* **Harry** *should hold it, and goes to* **Wesley**.

Nick   What's on *your* mind?

Wesley (*confused*)   Well –

Nick   Come on. Speak up. Are you hungry, or what?

Wesley   Honest to God, I ain't hungry. All I want is a job. I don't want no charity.

Nick   Well, what can you do, and how good are you?

Wesley   I can run errands, clean up, wash dishes, anything.

Dudley (*on the telephone, very eagerly*)   Elsie? Elsie, this is Dudley. Elsie, I'll jump in the bay if you don't marry me. Life isn't worth living without you. I can't sleep. I can't think of anything but you. All the time. Day and night and night and day. Elsie, I love you. I love you. What? (*Burning up.*) Is this Sunset 7-3-4-9? Pause.) 7943? (*Calmly, while* **Willie** *begins making a small racket.*) Well, what's *your* name? *Lorene?* Lorene Smith? I thought you were Elsie Mandelspiegel. What? Dudley. Yeah. Dudley R. Bostwick. Yeah. R. It stands for Raoul, but I never spell it out. I'm pleased to meet you, too. What? There's a lot of noise around here. (**Willie** *stops hitting the marble game.*) Where am I? At Nick's, on Pacific Street. I work at the SP. I told them I was sick and they gave me the afternoon off. Wait a minute. I'll ask them. I'd like to meet you, too. Sure. I'll ask them. (*Turns around to* **Nick**.) What's this address?

Nick   Number 3, Pacific Street, you cad.

Dudley   Cad? You don't know how I've been suffering on account of Elsie. I take things too ceremoniously. I've got to be more lackadaisical. (*Into telephone.*) Hello, Elenore? I mean, Lorene. It's Number 3 Pacific Street. Yeah. Sure. I'll wait for you. How'll you know me? You'll know me. I'll recognise *you*. Goodbye, now. (*He hangs up.*)

Harry (*continuing his monologue, with gestures, movements, and so on*) I'm standing there. I didn't do anything to anybody. Why should I be a soldier? (*Sincerely, insanely.*) BOOOOOOOM. WAR! OK. War. I retreat. I hate war. I move to Sacramento.

Nick (*shouting*)   All right, Comedian. Lay off a minute.

Harry (*broken-hearted, going to* **Willie**)   Nobody's got a sense of humour any more. The world's dying for comedy like never before, but nobody knows how to *laugh*.

Nick (*to* **Wesley**)   Do you belong to the union?

Wesley   What union?

Nick   For the love of Mike, where've you been? Don't you know you can't come into a place and ask for a job and get one and go to work, just like that. You've got to belong to one of the unions.

Wesley   I didn't know. I got to have a job. Real soon.

Nick   Well, you've got to belong to a union.

Wesley   I don't want any favours. All I want is a chance to earn a living.

Nick   Go on into the kitchen and tell Sam to give you some lunch.

Wesley   Honest, I ain't hungry.

Dudley (*shouting*)   What I've gone through for Elsie.

Harry   I've got all kinds of funny ideas in my head to help make the world happy again.

Nick (*holding* **Wesley**)   No, he isn't hungry.

Wesley *almost faints from hunger.* **Nick** *catches him just in time. The* **Arab** *and* **Nick** *go off with* **Wesley** *into the kitchen.*

Harry (*to* **Willie**)   See if you think this is funny. It's my own idea. I created this dance myself. It comes after the monologue.

Harry *begins to dance.* **Willie** *watches a moment, and then goes back to the game. It's a goofy dance, which* **Harry** *does with great sorrow, but much energy.*

Dudley   Elsie. Aw, gee, Elsie. What the hell do I want to see Lorene Smith for? Some girl I don't know.

Joe *and* **Kitty** *have been drinking in silence. There is no sound now except the soft-shoe shuffling of* **Harry**, *the comedian.*

Joe   What's the dream now, Kitty Duval?

Kitty (*dreaming the words and pictures*)   I dream of home. Christ, I always dream of home. I've no *home.* I've no place. But I always dream of all of us together again. We had a farm in Ohio. There was nothing good about it. It was always sad. There was always trouble. But I always dream about it as if I could go back and Papa would be there and Mamma and Louie and my little brother Stephen and my sister Mary. I'm Polish. Duval! My name isn't Duval, it's Koranovsky. Katerina Koranovsky. We lost everything. The house, the farm, the trees, the horses, the cows, the chickens. Papa died. He was old. He was thirteen years older than Mamma. We moved to Chicago. We tried to work. We tried to stay together. Louie got in trouble. The fellow he was with killed him for something. I don't know what. Stephen ran away from home. Seventeen years old. I don't know where he is. Then Mamma died. (*Pause.*) What's the dream? I dream of home.

Nick *comes out of the kitchen with* **Wesley**.

Nick   Here. Sit down and rest. That'll hold you for a *while*. Why didn't you tell me you were hungry? You all right now?

Wesley (*sitting down in the chair at the piano*)   Yes, I am. Thank you. I didn't know I was *that* hungry.

Nick   Fine. (*To* **Harry**, *who is dancing.*) Hey. What the hell do you think you're doing?

Harry (*stopping*)   That's my own idea. I'm a natural-born dancer and comedian.

Wesley *begins slowly, one note, one chord at a time, to play the piano.*

Nick   You're no good. Why don't you try some other kind of work? Why don't you get a job in a store, selling something? What do you want to be a comedian for?

Harry   I've got something for the world and they haven't got sense enough to let me give it to them. Nobody knows me.

Dudley   Elsie. Now I'm waiting for some dame I've never seen before. Lorene Smith. Never saw her in my life. Just happened to get the wrong number. She turns on the personality, and I'm a cooked Indian. Give me a beer, please.

Harry   Nick, you've got to see my act. It's the greatest thing of its kind in America. All I want is a chance. No salary to begin. Let me try it out tonight. If I don't wow 'em, OK, I'll go home. If vaudeville wasn't dead, a guy like me would have a chance.

Nick   You're not funny. You're a sad young punk. What the hell do you want to try to be funny for? You'll break everybody's heart. What's there for you to be funny about? You've been poor all your life, haven't you?

Harry   I've been poor all right, but don't forget that some things count more than some other things.

Nick   What counts more, for instance, than what else, for instance?

Harry   Talent, for instance, counts more than money, for instance, that's what, and I've got talent. I get new ideas night and day. Everything comes natural to me. I've got style, but it'll take me a little time to round it out. That's all.

By now **Wesley** *is playing something of his own which is very good and out of the world. He plays about half a minute, after which* **Harry** *begins to dance.*

Nick (*watching*)   I run the lousiest dive in Frisco, and a guy arrives and makes me stock up with champagne. The whores come in and holler at me that they're ladies. Talent comes in and begs me for a chance to show itself. Even society people come here once in a while. I don't know what for. Maybe it's liquor. Maybe it's the location. Maybe it's my personality. Maybe it's the crazy personality of the joint. The old honky-tonk. (*Pause.*) Maybe they can't feel at home anywhere else.

By now **Wesley** *is really playing, and* **Harry** *is going through a new routine.* **Dudley** *grows sadder and sadder.*

Kitty   Please dance with me.

Joe (*loudly*)   I never learned to dance.

Kitty   Anybody can dance. Just hold me in your arms.

Joe   I'm very fond of you. I'm *sorry*. I *can't* dance. I wish to God I could.

Kitty   Oh, please.

Joe   Forgive me. I'd like to very much.

Kitty *dances alone.* **Tom** *comes in with a package. He sees* **Kitty** *and goes gaga again. He comes out of the trance and puts the bundle on the table in front of* **Joe**.

Joe (*taking the package*)   What'd you get?

Tom   Two dollars' worth of toys. That's what you sent me for. The girl asked me what I wanted with toys. I didn't know what to tell her. (*He stares at* **Kitty**, *then back at* **Joe**.) Joe? I've got to have some money. After all you've done for me, I'll do anything in the world for you, but, Joe, you got to give me some money once in a while.

Joe   What do you want it for?

Tom *turns and stares at* **Kitty** *dancing.*

Joe (*noticing*)   Sure. Here. Here's five. (*Shouting.*) Can you dance?

Tom (*proudly*)   I got second prize at the Palomar in Sacramento five years ago.

Joe (*loudly, opening package*)   OK, dance with her.

Tom   You mean *her*?

Joe (*loudly*)   I mean Kitty Duval, the burlesque queen. I mean the queen of the world burlesque. Dance with her. She wants to dance.

Tom (*worshipping the name Kitty Duval, helplessly*)   Joe, can I tell you something?

Joe (*bringing out a toy and winding it*)   You don't have to. I know. You love her. You *really* love her. I'm not blind. I know. But take care of yourself. Don't get sick that way again.

Nick (*looking at and listening to* **Wesley** *with amazement*)   Comes in here and wants to be a dish-washer. Faints from hunger. And then sits down and plays better than Heifetz.

Joe   Heifetz plays the violin.

Nick   All right, don't get careful. He's good, ain't he?

Tom (*to* **Kitty**)   Kitty.

Joe (*he lets the toy go, loudly*)   Don't *talk*. Just dance.

Tom *and* **Kitty** *dance.* **Nick** *is at the bar, watching everything.* **Harry** *is dancing.* **Dudley** *is grieving into his beer.* **Lorene Smith**, *about thirty-seven, very overbearing and funny-looking, comes to the bar.*

Nick   What'll it be, lady?

Lorene (*looking about and scaring all the young men*)   I'm looking for the young man I talked to on the telephone. Dudley R. Bostwick.

Dudley (*jumping, running to her, stopping, shocked*)   Dudley R. (*Slowly.*) Bostwick? Oh, yeah. He left here ten minutes ago. You mean Dudley Bostwick, that poor man on crutches?

Lorene   Crutches?

Dudley   Yeah. Dudley Bostwick. That's what he *said* his name was. He said to tell you not to wait.

Lorene   Well. (*She begins to go, turns around.*) Are you sure *you're* not Dudley Bostwick?

Dudley   Who – me? (*Grandly.*) My name is Roger Tenefrancia. I'm a French-Canadian. I never saw the poor fellow before.

Lorene   It seems to me your voice is like the voice I heard over the telephone.

Dudley   A coincidence. An accident. A quirk of fate. One of those things. Dismiss the thought. That poor cripple hobbled out of here ten minutes ago.

Lorene   He said he was going to commit suicide. I only wanted to be of help. (*She goes.*)

Dudley   Be of help? What kind of help could she be of? (*He runs to the telephone in the corner.*) Gee whiz, Elsie. Gee whiz. I'll never leave you again. (*He turns the pages of a little address book.*) Why do I always forget the number? I've tried to get her on the phone a hundred times this week and I still forget the number. She won't come to the phone, but I keep trying anyway. She's out. She's not in. She's working. I get the wrong number. Everything goes haywire. I can't sleep. (*Defiantly.*) She'll come to the phone one of these days. If there's anything to true love at all, she'll come to the phone. Sunset 7349.

He dials the number, as **Joe** *goes on studying the toys. They are one big mechanical toy, whistles and a music box.* **Joe** *blows into the whistles, quickly, by way of getting casually acquainted with them.*

Tom *and* **Kitty** *stop dancing.* **Tom** *stares at her.*

Dudley   Hello. Is this Sunset 7349? May I speak to Elsie? Yes. (*Emphatically, and bitterly.*) No, this is *not* Dudley Bostwick. This is Roger Tenefrancia of Montreal, Canada. I'm a childhood friend of Miss Mandelspiegel. We went to kindergarten together. (*Hand over phone.*) Goddamnit. (*Into phone.*) Yes. I'll wait, thank you.

Tom   I love you.

Kitty   You want to go to my room?

Tom *can't answer.*

Kitty   Have you got two dollars?

Tom (*shaking his head with confusion*)   I've got *five* dollars, but I *love* you.

Kitty (*looking at him*)   You want to spend *all* that money?

Tom *embraces her. They go.* **Joe** *watches. Goes back to the toy.*

Joe   Where's that longshoreman, McCarthy?

Nick   He'll be around.

Joe   What do you think he'll have to say today?

Nick   Plenty, as usual. I'm going next door to see who won that third race at Laurel.

Joe   Precious Time won it.

Nick   That's what you think. (*He goes.*)

Joe (*to himself*)   A horse named McCarthy is running in the sixth race today.

Dudley (*on the phone*)   Hello. Hello. Elsie? Elsie? (*His voice weakens; also his limbs.*) My God. She's come to the phone. Elsie, I'm at Nick's on Pacific Street. You've got to come here and talk to me. Hello. Hello, Elsie? (*Amazed.*) Did she hang up? Or was I disconnected?

He hangs up and goes to the bar. **Wesley** *is still playing the piano.*

Harry *is still dancing.* **Joe** *has wound up the big mechanical toy and is watching it work.* **Nick** *returns.*

Nick (*watching the toy*)   Say. That's some gadget.

Joe   How much did I win?

Nick   How do you know you *won*?

Joe   Don't be silly. He said Precious Time was going to win by ten lengths, didn't he? He's in love, isn't he?

Nick   OK. I don't know why, but Precious Time won. You got eighty for ten. How do you do it?

Joe (*roaring*)   Faith. Faith. How'd he win?

Nick   By a nose. Look him up in the *Racing Form*. The slowest, the cheapest, the worst horse in the race, and the worst jockey. What's the matter with my luck?

Joe   How much did you lose?

Nick   Fifty cents.

Joe   You should never gamble.

Nick   Why not?

Joe   You always bet fifty cents. You've got no more faith than a flea, that's why.

Harry (*shouting*)   How do you like this, Nick? (*He is really busy now, all legs and arms.*)

Nick (*turning and watching*)   Not bad. Hang around. You can wait table. (*To* **Wesley***.*) Hey, Wesley. Can you play that again tonight?

Wesley (*turning, but still playing the piano*)   I don't know for sure, Mr Nick, I can play *something*.

Nick   Good. *You* hang around, too. (*He goes behind the bar.*)

The atmosphere is now one of warm, natural, American ease; every man innocent and good; each doing what he believes he should do, or what he must do. There is deep American naivety and faith in the behaviour of each person. No one is competing with anyone else. No one hates anyone else. Every man is living, and letting live. Each man is following his destiny as he feels it should be followed; or is abandoning it as he feels it must, by now, be abandoned; or is forgetting it for the moment as he feels he should forget it. Although everyone is dead serious, there is unmistakable smiling and humour in the scene; a sense of the human body and spirit emerging from the world-imposed state of stress and fretfulness, fear and awkwardness, to the natural state of casualness and grace. Each person belongs to the environment, in his own person, as himself. **Wesley** *is playing better than ever.* **Harry** *is hoofing better than ever.* **Nick** *is behind the bar shining glasses.* **Joe** *is smiling at the toy and studying it.* **Dudley**, *although still troubled, is at least calm now and full of melancholy poise.* **Willie**, *at the marble game, is happy. The* **Arab** *is deep in his memories, where he wants to be.*

Into this scene and atmosphere comes **Blick**.

Blick *is the sort of human being you dislike at sight. He is no different from anybody else physically. His face is an ordinary face. There is nothing obviously wrong with him, and yet you know that it is impossible, even by the most generous expansion of understanding, to accept him as a human being. He is the strong man without strength – strong only among the weak – the weakling who uses force on the weaker.*

Blick *enters casually, as if he were a customer, and immediately* **Harry** *begins slowing down.*

Blick (*oily, and with mock-friendliness*)   Hello, Nick.

Nick (*stopping his work and leaning across the bar*)   What do you want to come here for? You're too big a man for a little honky-tonk.

Blick (*flattered*)   Now, Nick.

Nick   Important people never come here. *Here.* Have a drink. (*Whiskey bottle.*)

Blick   Thanks, I don't drink.

Nick (*drinking the drink himself*)   Well, why don't you?

Blick   I have responsibilities.

Nick   You're head of the lousy Vice Squad. There's no vice here.

Blick (*sharply*)   Streetwalkers are working out of this place.

Nick (*angry*)   What do you want?

Blick (*loudly*)   I just want you to know that it's got to stop.

*The music stops. The mechanical toy runs down. There is absolute
silence, and a strange fearfulness and disharmony in the atmosphere now.*
Harry *doesn't know what to do with his hands or feet.* **Wesley**'s *arms
hang at his sides.* **Joe** *quietly pushes the toy to one side of the table, eager
to study what is happening.* **Willie** *stops playing the marble game, turns
around and begins to wait.* **Dudley** *straightens up very, very vigorously,
as if to say, 'Nothing can scare me. I know love is the only thing.' The*
Arab *is the same as ever, but watchful.* **Nick** *is arrogantly aloof. There
is a moment of silence and tension, as though* **Blick** *were waiting for
everybody to acknowledge his presence. He is obviously flattered by the
acknowledgement of* **Harry**, **Dudley**, **Wesley**, *and* **Willie**, *but
a little irritated by* **Nick**'s *aloofness and unfriendliness.*

Nick   Don't look at me. I can't tell a streetwalker from a lady.
You married?

Blick   You're not asking *me* questions. *I'm* telling you.

Nick (*interrupting*)   You're a man of about forty-five or so. You
ought to know better.

Blick (*angry*)   Streetwalkers are working out of this place.

Nick (*beginning to shout*)   Now, don't start any trouble with me.
People come here to drink and loaf around. I don't care who
they are.

Blick   Well, I do.

Nick   The only way to find out if a lady is a streetwalker is
to walk the streets with her, go to bed, and make sure. You
wouldn't want to do that. You'd *like* to, of course.

Blick   Any more of it, and I'll have your joint closed.

Nick (*very casually, without ill-will*)   Listen. I've got no use for
you, or anybody like you. You're out to change the world from
something bad to something worse. Something like yourself.

Blick (*furious pause, and contempt*)   I'll be back tonight. (*He begins to go.*)

Nick (*very angry but very calm*)   Do yourself a big favour and don't come back tonight. Send somebody else. I don't like your personality.

Blick (*casually, but with contempt*)   Don't break any laws. I don't like yours, either.

He looks the place over, and goes.

There is a moment of silence. Then **Willie** *turns and puts a new nickel in the slot and starts a new game.* **Wesley** *turns to the piano and rather falteringly begins to play. His heart really isn't in it.* **Harry** *walks about, unable to dance.* **Dudley** *lapses into his customary melancholy, at a table.* **Nick** *whistles a little; suddenly stops.* **Joe** *winds the toy.*

Joe (*comically*)   Nick. You going to kill that man?

Nick   I'm disgusted.

Joe   Yeah? Why?

Nick   Why should I get worked up over a guy like that? Why should I hate *him*? He's nothing. He's nobody. He's a mouse. But every time he comes into this place I get burned up. He doesn't want to drink. He doesn't want to sit down. He doesn't want to take things easy. Tell me one thing?

Joe   Do my best.

Nick   What's a punk like *that* want to go out and try to change the world for?

Joe (*amazed*)   Does *he* want to change the world, too?

Nick (*irritated*)   You know what I mean. What's he want to bother people for? He's *sick*.

Joe (*almost to himself, reflecting on the fact that* **Blick** *too wants to change the world*)   I guess he wants to change the world at that.

Nick   So I go to work and hate him.

Joe   It's not him, Nick. It's everything.

Nick   Yeah, I know. But I've still got no use for him. He's no good. You know what I mean? He hurts little people. (*Confused.*) One of the girls tried to commit suicide on account of him. (*Furiously.*) I'll break his head if he hurts anybody around here. This is my joint. (*Afterthought.*) Or anybody's *feelings*, either.

Joe   He may not be so bad, deep down underneath.

Nick   I know all about him. He's no good.

During this talk **Wesley** *has really begun to play the piano, the toy is rattling again and little by little* **Harry** *has begun to dance.* **Nick** *has come around the bar, and now, very much like a child – forgetting all his anger – is watching the toy work. He begins to smile at everything; turns and listens to* **Wesley***; watches* **Harry***; nods at the* **Arab***; shakes his head at* **Dudley***; and gestures amiably about* **Willie***. It's his joint all right. It's a good, low-down, honky-tonk American place that lets people alone.*

Nick   I've got a good joint. There's nothing wrong here. Hey. Comedian. Stick to the dancing tonight. I think you're OK. Wesley? Do some more of that tonight. That's fine!

Harry   Thanks, Nick. Gosh, I'm on my way at last. (*On telephone.*) Hello, Ma? Is that you, Ma? Harry. I got the job. (*He hangs up and walks around, smiling.*)

Nick (*watching the toy all this time*)   Say, that really is something. What is that, anyway?

Mary L *comes in.*

Joe (*holding it toward* **Nick** *and* **Mary L**)   Nick, this is a toy. A contraption devised by the cunning of man to drive boredom, or grief, or anger out of children. A noble gadget. A gadget, I might say, infinitely nobler than any other I can think of at the moment.

Everybody gathers around **Joe***'s table to look at the toy. The toy stops working.* **Joe** *winds the music box. Lifts a whistle; blows it, making a very strange, funny and sorrowful sound.*

Joe   Delightful. Tragic, but delightful.

Wesley *plays the music-box theme on the piano.* **Mary L** *takes a table.*

Nick   Joe. That girl, Kitty. What's she mean, calling me a dentist? I wouldn't hurt anybody, let alone a tooth.

Nick *goes to* **Mary L**'s *table.* **Harry** *imitates the toy. Dances. The piano music comes up, the light dims slowly, while the piano solo continues.*

Act Two

An hour later. All the people who were at **Nick***'s when the curtain came down are still there.* **Joe** *at his table, quietly shuffling and turning a pack of cards, and at the same time watching the face of* **Mary L***, and looking at the initials on her handbag, as though they were the symbols of the lost glory of the world.* **Mary L***, in turn, very casually regards* **Joe** *occasionally. Or rather senses him; has sensed him in fact the whole hour. She is mildly tight on beer, and* **Joe** *himself is tight, but as always completely under control; simply sharper. The others are about, at tables, and so on.*

Joe   Is it Madge – Laubowitz?

Mary   Is what what?

Joe   Is the name Mabel Lepescu?

Mary   What name?

Joe   The name the initials M.L. stand for. The initials on your bag.

Mary   No.

Joe   (*after a long pause, thinking deeply what the name might be, turning a card, looking into the beautiful face of the woman*)   Margie Longworthy?

Mary   (*all this is very natural and sincere, no comedy on the part of the people involved; they are both solemn, being drunk*)   No.

Joe   (*his voice higher pitched, as though he were growing a little alarmed*)   Midge Laurie?

Mary L *shakes her head*

Joe   My initials are J.T.

Mary   (*pause*)   John?

Joe   No. (*Pause.*) Martha Lancaster?

Mary   No. (*Slight pause.*) Joseph?

Joe   Well, not exactly. That's my first name, but everybody calls me Joe. The last name is the tough one. I'll help you a little. I'm Irish. (*Pause.*) Is it just plain Mary?

Mary   Yes, it is. I'm Irish, too. At least on my father's side. English on my mother's side.

Joe   I'm Irish on both sides. Mary's one of my favourite names. I guess that's why I didn't think of it. I met a girl in Mexico City named Mary once. She was an American from Philadelphia. She got married there. In Mexico City, I mean. While I was *there.* We were in love, too. At least I was. You never know about anyone else. They were engaged, you see, and her mother was with her, so they went through with it. Must have been six or seven years ago. She's probably got three or four children by this time.

Mary   Are you still in love with her?

Joe   Well – no. To tell you the truth, I'm not sure. I guess I am. I didn't even know she was engaged until a couple of days before they got married. I thought I was going to marry her. I kept thinking all the time about the kind of kids we would be likely to have. My favourite was the third one. The first two were fine. Handsome and fine and intelligent, but that third one was different. Dumb and goofy-looking. I liked *him* a lot. When she told me she was going to be married, I didn't feel so bad about the first two, it was that dumb one.

Mary (*after a pause of some few seconds*)   What do you do?

Joe   Do? To tell you the truth, nothing.

Mary   Do you always drink a great deal?

Joe (*scientifically*)   Not *always.* Only when I'm awake. I sleep seven or eight hours every night, you know.

Mary   How nice. I mean to drink when you're awake.

Joe (*thoughtfully*)   It's a privilege.

Mary   Do you really *like* to drink?

Joe (*positively*)   As much as I like to *breathe.*

Mary (*beautifully*)   Why?

Joe (*dramatically*)   Why do I like to drink? (*Pause.*) Because I don't like to be gypped. Because I don't like to be dead most of the time and just a little alive every once in a long while. (*Pause.*) If I don't drink, I become fascinated by unimportant things – like everybody else. I get busy. Do things. All kinds of little stupid things, for all kinds of little stupid reasons. Proud, selfish, *ordinary* things. I've done them. Now I don't do anything. *I live all the time.* Then I go to sleep.

Pause.

Mary   Do you sleep well?

Joe (*taking it for granted*)   Of course.

Mary (*quietly, almost with tenderness*)   What are your plans?

Joe (*loudly, but also tenderly*)   Plans? I haven't *got* any. *I just get up.*

Mary (*beginning to understand everything*)   Oh, yes. Yes, of course.

Dudley *puts a nickel in the phonograph.*

Joe (*thoughtfully*)   Why do I drink?

Pause, while he thinks about it. The thinking appears to be profound and complex, and has the effect of giving his face a very comical and naive expression.

That question calls for a pretty complicated answer. (*He smiles abstractedly.*)

Mary   Oh, I didn't mean –

Joe (*swiftly, gallantly*)   No. No. I *insist*. I *know* why. It's just a matter of finding words. Little ones.

Mary   It really doesn't matter.

Joe (*seriously*)   Oh, yes, it does. (*Clinically.*) Now, why do I drink? (*Scientifically.*) No. Why does *anybody* drink? (*Working it out.*) Every day has twenty-four hours.

Mary (*sadly, but brightly*)   Yes, that's true.

Joe   Twenty-four hours. Out of the twenty-four hours at *least* twenty-three and a half are − my God, I don't know why − dull, dead, boring, empty and murderous. Minutes on the clock, *not time of living.* It doesn't make any difference who you are or what you do, twenty-three and a half hours of the twenty-four are spent *waiting.*

Mary   Waiting?

Joe (*gesturing, loudly*)   And the more you wait, the less there is to wait *for.*

Mary (*attentively, beautifully his student*)   Oh?

Joe (*continuing*)   That goes on for days and days, and weeks and months and years, and years, and the first thing you know *all* the years are dead. All the minutes are dead. You yourself are dead. There's nothing to wait for any more. Nothing except *minutes* on the *clock.* No time of life. Nothing but minutes, and idiocy. Beautiful, bright, intelligent idiocy. (*Pause.*) Does that answer your question?

Mary (*earnestly*)   I'm afraid it does. Thank you. You shouldn't have gone to all the trouble.

Joe   No trouble at all. (*Pause.*) You have children?

Mary   Yes. Two. A son and a daughter.

Joe (*delighted*)   How swell. Do they look like you?

Mary   Yes.

Joe   Then why are you sad?

Mary   I was always sad. It's just that after I was married I was allowed to drink.

Joe (*eagerly*)   Who are you waiting for?

Mary   No one.

Joe (*smiling*)   I'm not waiting for anybody, either.

Mary   My husband, of course.

Joe   Oh, sure.

Mary   He's a lawyer.

Joe (*standing, leaning on the table*)   He's a great guy. I like him.
I'm very fond of him.

Mary (*listening*)   You have responsibilities?

Joe (*loudly*)   *One*, and *thousands.* As a matter of fact, I feel
responsible to everybody. At least to everybody I meet. I've
been trying for three years to find out if it's possible to live
what I think is a civilised life. I mean a life that can't hurt any
other life.

Mary   You're famous?

Joe   Very. Utterly unknown, but very famous. Would you like
to dance?

Mary   All right.

Joe (*loudly*)   I'm *sorry.* I don't dance. I didn't think you'd like to.

Mary   To tell you the truth, I don't like to dance at all.

Joe (*proudly; commentator*)   I can hardly walk.

Mary   You mean you're tight?

Joe (*smiling*)   No. I mean *all* the time.

Mary (*looking at him closely*)   Were you ever in Paris?

Joe   In 1929, and again in 1934.

Mary   What month of 1934?

Joe   Most of April, all of May, and a little of June.

Mary   I was there in November and December that year.

Joe   We were there almost at the same time. You were married?

Mary   Engaged.

They are silent a moment, looking at one another.

(*Quietly and with great charm.*) Are you really in love with me?

Joe   Yes.

Mary   Is it the champagne?

Joe   Yes. Partly, at least. (*He sits down.*)

Mary   If you don't see me again, will you be very unhappy?

Joe   Very.

Mary (*getting up*)   I'm so pleased.

Joe *is deeply grieved that she is going. In fact, he is almost panic-stricken about it, getting up in a way that is full of furious sorrow and regret.*

Mary   I must go now. Please don't get up.

Joe *is up, staring at her with amazement.*

Mary   Goodbye.

Joe (*simply*)   Goodbye.

The woman stands looking at him a moment, then turns and goes. **Joe** *stands staring after her for a long time. Just as he is slowly sitting down again, the* **Newsboy** *enters, and goes to* **Joe***'s table.*

Newsboy   Paper, Mister?

Joe   How many you got this time?

Newsboy   Eleven.

Joe *buys them all, looks at the lousy headlines, throws them away. The* **Newsboy** *looks at* **Joe**, *amazed. He walks over to* **Nick** *at the bar.*

Newsboy (*troubled*)   Hey, Mister, do you own this place?

Nick (*casually but emphatically*)   I own this place.

Newsboy   Can you use a great lyric tenor?

Nick (*almost to himself*)   Great lyric tenor? (*Loudly.*) Who?

Newsboy (*loud and the least bit angry*)   Me. I'm getting too big to sell papers. I don't want to holler headlines all the time. I want to *sing*. You can use a great lyric tenor, can't you?

Nick   What's lyric about you?

Newsboy (*voice high-pitched, confused*)   My voice.

Nick   Oh. (*Slight pause, giving in.*) All right, then – sing!

The **Newsboy** *breaks into swift and beautiful song: 'When Irish Eyes Are Smiling'.* **Nick** *and* **Joe** *listen carefully;* **Nick** *with wonder,* **Joe** *with amazement and delight.*

Newsboy (*singing*)
> When Irish eyes are smiling,
> Sure 'tis like a morn in spring.
> In the lilt of Irish laughter,
> You can hear the angels sing.
> When Irish hearts are happy,
> All the world seems bright and gay.
> But when Irish eyes are smiling –

Nick (*loudly, swiftly*)   Are you Irish?

Newsboy (*speaking swiftly, loudly, a little impatient with the irrelevant question*)   No. I'm Greek.

He finishes the song, singing louder than ever.

> Sure they steal your heart away.

He turns to **Nick** *dramatically, like a vaudeville singer begging his audience for applause.* **Nick** *studies the boy eagerly.* **Joe** *gets to his feet and leans toward the* **Newsboy** *and* **Nick**.

Nick   Not bad. Let me hear you again about a year from now.

Newsboy (*thrilled*)   Honest?

Nick   Yeah. Along about 7th November 1940.

Newsboy (*happier than ever before in his life, running over to* **Joe**) Did you hear it too, Mister?

Joe   Yes, and it's great. What part of Greece?

Newsboy   Salonika. Gosh, Mister. Thanks.

Joe   Don't wait a year. Come back with some papers a little later. You're a great singer.

Newsboy (*thrilled and excited*)   Aw, thanks, Mister. So long. (*Running to* **Nick**.) Thanks, Mister.

He runs out. **Joe** *and* **Nick** *look at the swinging doors.* **Joe** *sits down.* **Nick** *laughs.*

Nick   Joe, people are so wonderful. Look at that kid.

Joe   Of course they're wonderful. Every one of them is wonderful.

McCarthy *and* **Krupp** *come in, talking.*

McCarthy *is a big man in work clothes, which make him seem very young. He is wearing black jeans, and a blue workman's shirt. No tie. No hat. He has broad shoulders, a lean intelligent face, thick black hair. In his right back pocket is the longshoreman's hook. His arms are long and hairy. His sleeves are rolled up to just below his elbows. He is a casual man, easy-going in movement, sharp in perception, swift in appreciation of charm or innocence or comedy, and gentle in spirit, His speech is clear and full of warmth. His voice is powerful, but modulated. He enjoys the world, in spite of the mess it is, and he is fond of people, in spite of the mess they are.*

Krupp *is not quite as tall or broad-shouldered as* **McCarthy**. *He is physically encumbered by his uniform, club, pistol, belt and cap. And he is plainly not at home in the role of policeman. His movement is stiff and unintentionally pompous. He is a naive man, essentially good. His understanding is less than* **McCarthy**'s, *but he is honest and he doesn't try to bluff.*

Krupp   You don't understand what I mean. Hi-ya, Joe.

Joe   Hello, Krupp.

McCarthy   Hi-ya, Joe.

Joe   Hello, McCarthy.

Krupp   Two beers, Nick. (*To* **McCarthy**.) All I do is carry out orders, carry out orders. I don't know what the idea is behind the order. Who it's for, or who it's against, or why. All I do is carry it out.

Nick *gives them beer.*

McCarthy   You don't read enough.

Krupp   I do read. I read the *Examiner* every morning. The *Call-Bulletin* every night.

McCarthy   And carry out orders. What are the orders now?

Krupp   To keep the peace down here on the waterfront.

McCarthy   Keep it for who? (*To* **Joe**.) Right?

Joe (*sorrowfully*)   Right.

Krupp   How do I know for who? The peace. Just keep it.

McCarthy   It's got to be kept for somebody. Who would you suspect it's kept for?

Krupp   For citizens!

McCarthy   I'm a citizen!

Krupp   All right, I'm keeping it for you.

McCarthy   By hitting me over the head with a club? (*To* **Joe**.) Right?

Joe (*melancholy, with remembrance*)   I don't know.

Krupp   Mac, you know I never hit you over the head with a club.

McCarthy   But you will if you're on duty at the time and happen to stand on the opposite side of myself, on duty.

Krupp   We went to Mission High together. We were always good friends. The only time we ever fought was that time over Alma Haggerty. Did you marry Alma Haggerty? (*To* **Joe**.) Right?

Joe   Everything's right.

McCarthy   No. Did you? (*To* **Joe**.) Joe, are you with me or against me?

Joe   I'm with everybody. One at a time.

Krupp   No. And that's just what I mean.

McCarthy   You mean neither one of us is going to marry the thing we're fighting for?

Krupp   *I don't even know what it is.*

McCarthy   You don't read enough, I tell you.

Krupp   Mac, you don't know what you're fighting for, either.

McCarthy   It's so simple, it's fantastic.

Krupp   All right, what are you fighting for?

McCarthy   For the rights of the inferior. Right?

Joe   Something like that.

Krupp   The who?

McCarthy   The inferior. The world full of Mahoneys who haven't got what it takes to make monkeys out of everybody else near by. The men who were created equal. Remember?

Krupp   Mac, you're not inferior.

McCarthy   I'm a longshoreman. And an idealist. I'm a man with too much brawn to be an intellectual, exclusively. I married a small, sensitive, cultured woman so that my kids would be sissies instead of suckers. A strong man with any sensibility has no choice in this world but to be a heel, or a *worker*. I haven't the heart to be a heel, so I'm a worker. I've got a son in high school who's already thinking of being a writer.

Krupp   I wanted to be a writer once.

Joe   Wonderful. (*He puts down the paper, looks at* **Krupp** *and* **McCarthy**.)

McCarthy   They *all* wanted to be writers. Every maniac in the world that ever brought about the murder of people through war started out in an attic or basement writing poetry. It stank. So they get even by becoming important heels. And it's still going on.

Krupp   Is it really, Joe?

Joe   Look at today's paper.

McCarthy   Right now on Telegraph Hill is some punk who is trying to be Shakespeare. Ten years from now he'll be a senator. Or a communist.

Krupp   Somebody ought to do something about it.

McCarthy (*mischievously, with laughter in his voice*)   The thing to do is to have more magazines. Hundreds of them. *Thousands.* Print everything they write, so they'll believe they're immortal. That may keep them from going haywire.

Krupp   Mac, you ought to be a writer yourself.

McCarthy   I hate the tribe. They're mischief-makers. Right?

Joe (*swiftly*)   Everything's right. Right and wrong.

Krupp   Then why do you read?

McCarthy (*laughing*)   It's relaxing. It's soothing. (*Pause.*) The lousiest people born into the world are writers. Language is all right. It's the people who use language that are lousy.

*The **Arab** has moved a little closer, and is listening carefully.*

McCarthy (*to the **Arab***)   What do you think, Brother?

Arab (*after making many faces, thinking very deeply*)   No foundation. All the way down the line. What. What-not. Nothing. I go walk and look at sky. (*He goes.*)

Krupp   What? What-not? (*To **Joe**.*) What's that mean?

Joe (*slowly, thinking, remembering*)   What? What-not? That means this side, that side. Inhale, exhale. What: birth. What-not: death. The inevitable, the astounding, the magnificent seed of growth and decay in all things. Beginning, and end. That man, in his own way, is a prophet. He is one who, with the help of *beer*, is able to reach that state of deep understanding in which what and what-not, the reasonable and the unreasonable, are *one*.

McCarthy   Right.

Krupp   If you can understand that kind of talk, how can you be a longshoreman?

McCarthy   I come from a long line of McCarthys who never married or slept with anything but the most powerful and quarrelsome flesh. (*He drinks beer.*)

Krupp   I could listen to you two guys for hours, but I'll be damned if I know what the hell you're talking about.

McCarthy   The consequence is that all the McCarthys are too great and too strong to be heroes. Only the weak and unsure perform the heroic. They've *got* to. The more heroes you have, the worse the history of the world becomes. Right?

Joe   Go outside and look at it.

Krupp   You can sure philos – philosoph – Boy, you can talk.

McCarthy   I wouldn't talk this way to anyone but a man in uniform, and a man who couldn't understand a word of what I was saying. The party I'm speaking of, my friend, is *you*.

The phone rings. **Harry** *gets up from his table suddenly and begins a new dance.*

Krupp (*noticing him, with great authority*)   Here. Here. What do you think you're doing?

Harry (*stopping*)   I just got an idea for a new dance. I'm trying it out. Nick. Nick, the phone's ringing.

Krupp (*to* **McCarthy**)   Has he got a right to do that?

McCarthy   The living have danced from the beginning of time. I might even say, the dance and the life have moved along together, until now we have – (*To* **Harry**.) Go into your dance, son, and show us what we have.

Harry   I haven't got it worked out *completely* yet, but it starts out like this. (*He dances.*)

Nick (*on phone*)   Nick's Pacific Street Restaurant, Saloon and Entertainment Palace. Good afternoon. Nick speaking. (*Listens.*) Who? (*Turns around.*) Is there a Dudley Bostwick in the joint?

Dudley *jumps to his feet and goes to phone.*

Dudley (*on phone*)   Hello. Elsie? (*Listens.*) You're coming down? (*Elated. To the saloon.*) She's coming down. (*Pause.*) No. I won't drink. Aw, gosh, Elsie.

He hangs up, looks about him strangely, as if he were just born, walks around touching things, putting chairs in place, and so on.

McCarthy (*to* **Harry**)   Splendid. Splendid.

Harry   Then I go into this little routine. (*He demonstrates.*)

Krupp   Is that good, Mac?

McCarthy   It's awful, but it's honest and ambitious, like everything else in this great country.

Harry   Then I work along into this. (*He demonstrates.*) And *this* is where I *really* get going. (*He finishes the dance.*)

McCarthy   Excellent. A most satisfying demonstration of the present state of the American body and soul. Son, you're a genius.

Harry (*delighted, shaking hands with* **McCarthy**)   I go in front of an audience for the first time in my life tonight.

McCarthy   They'll be delighted. Where'd you learn to dance?

Harry   Never took a lesson in my life. I'm a natural-born dancer. And *comedian* too.

McCarthy (*astounded*)   You can make people *laugh*?

Harry (*dumbly*)   I can be funny, but they won't laugh.

McCarthy   That's odd. Why not?

Harry   I don't know. They just won't laugh.

McCarthy   Would you care to be funny now?

Harry   I'd like to try out a new monologue I've been thinking about.

McCarthy   Please do. I promise you if it's funny I shall *roar* with laughter.

Harry   This is it. (*Goes into the act, with much energy.*) I'm up at
Sharkey's on Turk Street. It's a quarter to nine, daylight saving.
Wednesday, the eleventh. What I've got is a headache and a
1918 nickel. What I *want* is a cup of coffee. If I buy a cup of
coffee with the nickel, I've got to walk home. I've got an
eight-ball problem. George the Greek is shooting a game of
snooker with Pedro the Filipino. *I'm in rags.* They're wearing
thirty-five-dollar suits, made to order. I haven't got a cigarette.
They're smoking Bobby Burns panatellas. I'm thinking it over,
like I always do. George the Greek is in a tough spot. If I buy
a cup of coffee, I'll want another cup. What happens? My *ear*
aches! My ear. George the Greek takes the cue. Chalks it.
Studies the table. Touches the cue ball delicately. Tick. What
happens? He makes the three-ball! What do I do? I get confused.
I go out and buy a morning paper. What the hell do I want with a
morning paper? What I *want* is a cup of coffee, and a good
used car. I go out and buy a moming paper. Thursday, the
twelfth, maybe the headline's about *me.* I take a quick look. No.
The headline is not about me. It's about Hitler. Seven thousand
miles away. I'm here. Who the hell is Hitler? Who's behind the
eight-ball? I turn around. Everybody's behind the eight-ball!

Pause. **Krupp** *moves toward* **Harry** *as if to make an important arrest.*
Harry *moves to the swinging doors.* **McCarthy** *stops* **Krupp.**

McCarthy (*to* **Harry**)   It's the funniest thing I've ever heard.
Or *seen*, for that matter.

Harry (*coming back to* **McCarthy**)   Then, why don't you laugh?

McCarthy   I don't know, *yet.*

Harry   I'm always getting funny ideas that nobody will laugh
at.

McCarthy (*thoughtfully*)   It may be that you've stumbled
headlong into a new kind of comedy.

Harry   Well, what good is it if it doesn't make anybody
laugh?

McCarthy   There are *kinds* of laughter, son. I must say, in all
truth, that I *am* laughing, although not out *loud.*

Harry   I want to *hear* people laugh. *Out loud.* That's why I keep thinking of funny things to say.

McCarthy   Well. They may catch on in time. Let's go, Krupp. So long, Joe.

McCarthy *and* **Krupp** *go.*

Joe   So long. (*After a moment's pause.*) Hey, Nick.

Nick   Yeah.

Joe   Bet McCarthy in the last race.

Nick   You're crazy. That horse is a double-crossing, no-good –

Joe   Bet everything you've got on McCarthy.

Nick   I'm not betting a nickel on him. *You* bet everything you've got on McCarthy.

Joe   I don't need money.

Nick   What makes you think McCarthy's going to win?

Joe   McCarthy's name's McCarthy, isn't it?

Nick   Yeah. So what?

Joe   The *horse* named McCarthy is going to win, *that's all.* Today.

Nick   Why?

Joe   You do what I tell you, and everything will be all right.

Nick   McCarthy likes to talk, that's all. (*Pause.*) Where's Tom?

Joe   He'll be around. He'll be miserable, but he'll be around. Five or ten minutes more.

Nick   You don't believe that Kitty, do you? About being in burlesque?

Joe (*very clearly*)   I believe dreams sooner than statistics.

Nick (*remembering*)   She sure is somebody. Called me a dentist.

Tom, *turning about, confused, troubled, comes in, and hurries to* **Joe**'s *table.*

Joe   What's the matter?

Tom   Here's your five, Joe. I'm in trouble again.

Joe   If it's not organic, it'll cure itself. If it is organic, science will cure it. What is it, organic or non-organic?

Tom   Joe, I don't know – (*He seems to be completely broken-down.*)

Joe   What's eating you? I want you to go on an errand for me.

Tom   It's Kitty.

Joe   What about her?

Tom   She's up in her room, crying.

Joe   Crying?

Tom   Yeah, she's been crying for over an hour. I been talking to her all this time, but she won't stop.

Joe   What's she crying about?

Tom   I don't know. I couldn't understand anything. She kept crying and telling me about a big house and collie dogs all around and flowers and one of her brothers dead and the other one lost somewhere. Joe, I can't stand Kitty crying.

Joe   You want to marry the girl?

Tom (*nodding*)   Yeah.

Joe (*curious and sincere*)   Why?

Tom   I don't know why, exactly, Joe. (*Pause.*) Joe, I don't like to think of Kitty out in the streets. I guess I love her, that's all.

Joe   She's a nice girl.

Tom   She's like an angel. She's not like those other streetwalkers.

Joe (*swiftly*)   Here. Take all this money and run next door to Frankie's and bet it on the nose of McCarthy.

Tom (swiftly)   All this money, Joe? McCarthy?

Joe   Yeah. Hurry.

Tom (*going*)   Ah, Joe. If McCarthy wins we'll be rich.

Joe   Get going, will you?

Tom *runs out and nearly knocks over the* **Arab** *coming back in.* **Nick** *fills him a beer without a word.*

Arab   No foundation, anywhere. Whole world. No foundation. All the way down the line.

Nick (*angry*)   McCarthy! Just because you got a little lucky this morning, you have to go to work and throw away eighty bucks.

Joe   He wants to marry her.

Nick   Suppose she doesn't want to marry *him*?

Joe (*amazed*)   Oh yeah. (*Thinking*) Now, why wouldn't she want to marry a nice guy like Tom?

Nick   She's been in burlesque. She's had flowers sent to her by European royalty. She's dined with young men of quality and social position. She's above Tom.

Tom *comes running in.*

Tom (*disgusted*)   They were running when I got there. Frankie wouldn't take the bet. McCarthy didn't get a call till the stretch. I thought we were going to save all this money. Then McCarthy won by *two* lengths.

Joe   What'd he pay, fifteen to one?

Tom   Better, but Frankie wouldn't take the bet.

Nick (*throwing a dish towel across the room*)   Well, for the love of Mike.

Joe   Give me the money.

Tom (*giving back the money*)   We would have had about a thousand five hundred dollars.

Joe (*bored, casually, inventing*)   Go up to Schwabacher-Frey and get me the biggest Rand-McNally map of the nations of

Europe they've got. On your way back stop at one of the pawn shops on Third Street, and buy me a good revolver and some cartridges.

Tom   She's up in her room crying, Joe.

Joe   Go get me those things.

Nick   What are you going to do, study the map, and then go out and shoot somebody?

Joe   I want to read the names of some European towns and rivers and valleys and mountains.

Nick   What do you want with the revolver?

Joe   I want to study it. I'm interested in things. Here's twenty dollars, Tom. Now go get them things.

Tom   A big map of Europe. And a revolver.

Joe   Get a good one. Tell the man you don't know anything about firearms and you're trusting him not to fool you. Don't pay more than ten dollars.

Tom   Joe, you got something on your mind. Don't go fool with a revolver.

Joe   Be sure it's a good one.

Tom   Joe.

Joe (*irritated*)   What, Tom?

Tom   Joe, what do you send me out for crazy things for all the time?

Joe (*angry*)   They're not crazy, Tom. Now, get going.

Tom   What about Kitty, Joe?

Joe   Let her cry. It'll do her good.

Tom   If she comes in here while I'm gone, talk to her, will you, Joe? Tell her about me.

Joe   OK. Get going. Don't load that gun. Just buy it and bring it here.

Tom (*going*)   You won't catch me loading any gun.

Joe   Wait a minute. Take these toys away.

Tom   Where'll I take them?

Joe   Give them to some kid. (*Pause.*) No. Take them up to Kitty. Toys stopped me from crying once. That's the reason I had you buy them. I wanted to see if I could find out *why* they stopped me from crying. I remember they seemed awfully stupid at the time.

Tom   Shall I, Joe? Take them up to Kitty? Do you think they'd stop *her* from crying?

Joe   They might. You get curious about the way they work and you forget whatever it is you're remembering that's making you cry. That's what they're for.

Tom   Yeah. Sure. The girl at the store asked me what I wanted with toys. I'll take them up to Kitty. (*Tragically.*) She's like a little girl. (*He goes.*)

Wesley   Mr Nick, can I play the piano again?

Nick   Sure. Practise all you like – until I tell you to stop.

Wesley   You going to pay me for playing the piano?

Nick   Sure. I'll give you enough to get by on.

Wesley (*amazed and delighted*)   Get money for playing the piano?

He goes to the piano and begins to play quietly. **Harry** *goes up on the little stage and listens to the music. After a while he begins a soft-shoe dance.*

Nick   What were you crying about?

Joe   My mother.

Nick   What about her?

Joe   She was dead. I stopped crying when they gave me the toys.

Nick's *mother, a little old woman of sixty or so, dressed plainly in black, her face shining, comes in briskly, chattering loudly in Italian, gesturing.* **Nick** *is delighted to see her.*

Ma (*in Italian*)   Everything all right, Nickie?

Nick (*in Italian*)   Sure, Mamma.

Ma *leaves as gaily and as noisily as she came, after half a minute of loud Italian family talk.*

Joe   Who was that?

Nick (*to* **Joe**, *proudly and a little sadly*)   My mother. (*Still looking at the swinging doors.*)

Joe   What'd she say?

Nick   Nothing. Just wanted to see me. (*Pause.*) What do you want with that gun?

Joe   I study things, Nick.

An old man who looks as if he might have been **Kit Carson** *at one time, walks in importantly, moves about, and finally stands at* **Joe**'s *table.*

Kit Carson   Murphy's the name. Just an old trapper. Mind if I sit down?

Joe   Be delighted. What'll you drink?

Kit Carson (*sitting down*)   Beer. Same as I've been drinking. And thanks.

Joe (*to* **Nick**)   Glass of beer, Nick.

Nick *brings the beer to the table,* **Kit Carson** *swallows it in one swig, wipes his big white moustache with the back of his right hand.*

Kit Carson (*moving in*)   I don't suppose you ever fell in love with a midget weighing thirty-nine pounds?

Joe (*studying the man*)   Can't say I have, but have another beer.

Kit Carson (*intimately*)   Thanks, thanks. Down in Gallup, twenty years ago. Fellow by the name of Rufus Jenkins came to town with six white horses and two black ones. Said he wanted a man to break the horses for him because his left leg was wood and he couldn't do it. Had a meeting at Parker's Mercantile Store and finally came to blows, me and Henry Walpal. Bashed his head with a brass cuspidor and ran away to Mexico, but he didn't die.

Couldn't speak a word. Took up with a cattle-breeder named Diego, educated in California. Spoke the language better than you and me. Said, Your job, Murph, is to feed them prize bulls. I said, Fine, what'll I feed them? He said, Hay, lettuce, salt, beer and aspirin.

Came to blows two days later over an accordion he claimed I stole. I had *borrowed* it. During the fight I busted it over his head; ruined one of the finest accordions I ever saw. Grabbed a horse and rode back across the border. Texas. Got to talking with a fellow who looked honest. Turned out to be a Ranger who was looking for me.

Joe   Yeah. You were saying, a thirty-nine-pound midget.

Kit Carson   Will I ever forget that lady? Will I ever get over that amazon of small proportions?

Joe   Will you?

Kit Carson   If I live to be sixty.

Joe   Sixty? You look more than sixty now.

Kit Carson   That's trouble showing in my face. Trouble and complications. I was fifty-eight three months ago.

Joe   That accounts for it, then. Go ahead, tell me more.

Kit Carson   Told the Texas Ranger my name was Rothstein, mining engineer from Pennsylvania, looking for something worthwhile. Mentioned two places in Houston. Nearly lost an eye early one morning, going down the stairs. Ran into a six-footer with an iron claw where his right hand was supposed to be. Said, You broke up my home. Told him I was a stranger to Houston. The girls gathered at the top of the stairs to see a fight. Seven of them. Six feet and an iron claw. That's bad on the nerves. Kicked him in the mouth when he swung for my head with the claw. Would have lost an eye except for quick thinking. He rolled into the gutter and pulled a gun. Fired seven times, I was back upstairs. Left the place an hour later, dressed in silk and feathers, with a hat swung around over my face. Saw him standing on the corner, waiting. Said, Care for a wiggle? Said he didn't. I went on down the street and left town. I don't suppose you ever had to put a dress on to save your skin, did you?

Joe   No, and I never fell in love with a midget weighing thirty-nine pounds. Have another beer?

Kit Carson   Thanks. (*Swallows glass of beer.*) Ever try to herd cattle on a bicycle?

Joe   No. I never got around to that.

Kit Carson   Left Houston with sixty cents in my pocket, gift of a girl named Lucinda. Walked fourteen miles in fourteen hours. Big house with barbwire all around, and big dogs. One thing I never could get around. Walked past the gate, anyway, from hunger and thirst. Dogs jumped up and came for me. Walked right into them, growing older every second. Went up to the door and knocked. Big Negress opened the door, closed it quick. Said, On your way, white trash.

Knocked again. Said, On your way. Again. On your way. Again. This time the old man himself opened the door, ninety, if he was a day. Sawed-off shotgun, too.

Said, I ain't looking for trouble, Father. I'm hungry and thirsty, name's Cavanaugh.

Took me in and made mint juleps for the two of us.

Said, Living here alone, Father?

Said, Drink and ask no questions. Maybe I am and maybe I ain't. You saw the lady. Draw your own conclusions.

I'd heard of that, but didn't wink out of tact. If I told you that old Southern gentleman was my grandfather, you wouldn't believe me, would you?

Joe   I might.

Kit Carson   Well, it so happens he wasn't. Would have been romantic if he had been, though.

Joe   Where did you herd cattle on a bicycle?

Kit Carson   Toledo, Ohio, 1918.

Joe   Toledo, Ohio? They don't herd cattle in Toledo.

Kit Carson   They don't any more. They did in 1918. One fellow did, leastaways. Bookkeeper named Sam Gold. Straight from the East Side, New York. Sombrero, lariats, Bill Durham, two head of cattle and two bicycles. Called his place the Gold Bar Ranch, two acres, just outside the city limits. That was the year of the war, you'll remember.

Joe   Yeah, I remember, but how about herding them two cows on a bicycle? How'd you do it?

Kit Carson   Easiest thing in the world. Rode no hands. Had to, otherwise couldn't lasso the cows. Worked for Sam Gold till the cows ran away. Bicycles scared them. They went into Toledo. Never saw hide nor hair of them again. Advertised in every paper, but never got them back. Broke his heart. Sold both bikes and returned to New York.

Took four aces from a pack of red cards and walked to town. Poker. Fellow in the game named Chuck Collins, liked to gamble. Told him with a smile I didn't suppose he'd care to bet a hundred dollars I wouldn't hold four aces the next hand. Called it. My cards were red on the blank side. The other cards were blue. Plumb forgot all about it. Showed him four aces. Ace of spades, ace of clubs, ace of diamonds, ace of hearts. I'll remember them four cards if I live to be sixty. Would have been killed on the spot except for the hurricane that year.

Joe   Hurricane?

Kit Carson   You haven't forgotten the Toledo hurricane of 1918, have you?

Joe   No. There was no hurricane in Toledo in 1918, or any other year.

Kit Carson   For the love of God, then what do you suppose that commotion was? And how come I came to in Chicago, dream-walking down State Street?

Joe   I guess they scared you.

Kit Carson   No, that wasn't it. You go back to the papers of November 1918, and I think you'll find there was a hurricane in Toledo. I remember sitting on the roof of a two-storey house, floating north-west.

Joe (*seriously*)   North-west?

Kit Carson   Now, son, don't tell me *you* don't believe me, either?

Pause.

Joe (*very seriously, energetically and sharply*)   Of course I believe you. Living is an art. It's not bookkeeping. It takes a lot of rehearsing for a man to get to be himself.

Kit Carson (*thoughtfully, smiling, and amazed*)   You're the first man I've ever met who believes me.

Joe (*seriously*)   Have another beer.

Tom *comes in with the Rand-McNally book, the revolver and the box of cartridges.* **Kit Carson** *goes to bar.*

Joe (*to* **Tom**)   Did you give her the toys?

Tom   Yeah, I gave them to her.

Joe   Did she stop crying?

Tom   No. She started crying harder than ever.

Joe   That's funny. I wonder why.

Tom   Joe, if I was a minute earlier, Frankie would have taken the bet and now we'd have about a thousand five hundred dollars. How much of it would you have given me, Joe?

Joe   If she'd marry you – *all* of it.

Tom   Would you, Joe?

Joe (*opening packages, examining book first, and revolver next*)   Sure. In this realm there's only one subject, and you're it. It's my duty to see that my subject is happy.

Tom   Joe, do you think we'll ever have eighty dollars for a race sometime again when there's a fifteen-to-one shot that we like, weather good, track fast, they get off to a good start, our horse doesn't get a call till the stretch, we think we're going to lose all that money, and then it wins, by a nose?

Joe   I didn't quite get that.

Tom   You know what I mean.

Joe   You mean the impossible. No, Tom, we won't. We were just a little late, that's all.

Tom   We might, Joe.

Joe   It's not likely.

Tom   Then how am I ever going to make enough money to marry her?

Joe   I don't know, Tom. Maybe you aren't.

Tom   Joe, I got to marry Kitty. (*Shaking his head.*) You ought to see the crazy room she lives in.

Joe   What kind of a room is it?

Tom   It's little. It crowds you in. It's bad, Joe. Kitty don't belong in a place like that.

Joe   You want to take her away from there?

Tom   Yeah. I want her to live in a house where there's room enough to live. Kitty ought to have a garden, or something.

Joe   You want to take care of her?

Tom   Yeah, sure, Joe. I ought to take care of somebody good that makes me feel like *I'm* somebody.

Joe   That means you'll have to get a job. What can you do?

Tom   I finished high school, but I don't know what I can do.

Joe   Sometimes when you think about it, what do you think you'd like to do?

Tom   Just sit around like you, Joe, and have somebody run errands for me and drink champagne and take things easy and never be broke and never worry about money.

Joe   That's a noble ambition.

Nick (*to* **Joe**)   How do you do it?

Joe   I really don't know, but I think you've got to have the full cooperation of the Good Lord.

Nick   I can't understand the way you talk.

Tom   Joe, shall I go back and see if I can get her to stop crying?

Joe   Give me a hand and I'll go with you.

Tom (*amazed*)   What! You're going to get up already?

Joe   She's crying, isn't she?

Tom   She's crying. Worse than ever now.

Joe   I thought the toys would stop her.

Tom   I've seen you sit in one place from four in the morning till two the next morning.

Joe   At my best, Tom, I don't travel by foot. That's all. Come on. Give me a hand. I'll find some way to stop her from crying.

Tom (*helping* **Joe**)   Joe, I never did tell you. You're a different kind of a guy.

Joe (*swiftly, a little angry*)   Don't be silly. I don't understand things. I'm trying to understand them.

Joe *is a little drunk. They go out together. The lights go down slowly, while* **Wesley** *plays the piano, and come up slowly on:*

Act Three

A cheap bed in Nick's to indicate Room 21 of the New York Hotel, upstairs, around the corner from Nick's. The bed can be at the centre of Nick's, or upon the little stage. Everything in Nick's is the same, except that all the people are silent, immobile and in darkness, except **Wesley** *who is playing the piano softly and sadly.* **Kitty Duval,** *in a dress she has carried around with her from the early days in Ohio, is seated on the bed, tying a ribbon in her hair. She looks at herself in a hand mirror. She is deeply grieved at the change she sees in herself. She takes off the ribbon, angry and hurt. She lifts a book from the bed and tries to read. She begins to sob again. She picks up an old picture of herself and looks at it. Sobs harder than ever, falling on the bed and burying her face. There is a knock, as if at the door.*

Kitty (*sobbing*)   Who is it?

Tom's voice   Kitty, it's me. Tom. Me and Joe.

Joe, *followed by* **Tom,** *comes to the bed quietly.* **Joe** *is holding a rather large toy carousel. He studies* **Kitty** *a moment. He sets the toy carousel on the floor, at the foot of* **Kitty**'s *bed.*

Tom (*standing over* **Kitty** *and bending down close to her*)   Don't cry any more, Kitty.

Kitty (*not looking, sobbing*)   I don't like this life.

Joe *starts the carousel which makes a strange, sorrowful, tinkling music. The music begins slowly, becomes swift, gradually slows down and ends.* **Joe** *himself is interested in the toy, watches and listens to it carefully.*

Tom (*eagerly*)   Kitty. Joe got up from his chair at Nick's just to get you a toy and come here. This one makes music. We rode all over town in a cab to get it. Listen.

Kitty *sits up slowly, listening, while* **Tom** *watches her. Everything happens slowly and sombrely.* **Kitty** *notices the photograph of herself when she was a little girl. Lifts it, and looks at it again.*

Tom (*looking*)   Who's that little girl, Kitty?

Kitty   That's me. When I was seven.

She hands the photo to **Tom**.

Tom (*looking, smiling*)   Gee, you're pretty, Kitty.

Joe *reaches up for the photograph, which* **Tom** *hands to him.* **Tom** *returns to* **Kitty**, *whom he finds as pretty now as she was at seven.* **Joe** *studies the photograph.* **Kitty** *looks up at* **Tom**. *There is no doubt that they really love one another.* **Joe** *looks up at them.*

Kitty   Tom?

Tom (*eagerly*)   Yeah, Kitty.

Kitty   Tom, when you were a little boy what did you want to be?

Tom (*a little bewildered, but eager to please her*)   What, Kitty?

Kitty   Do you remember when you were a little boy?

Tom (*thoughtfully*)   Yeah, I remember sometimes, Kitty.

Kitty   What did you want to be?

Tom *looks at* **Joe**. **Joe** *holds* **Tom**'*s eyes a moment. Then* **Tom** *is able to speak.*

Tom   Sometimes I wanted to be locomotive engineer. Sometimes I wanted to be a policeman.

Kitty   I wanted to be a great actress. (*She looks up into* **Tom**'*s face.*) Tom, didn't you ever want to be a doctor?

Tom *looks at* **Joe**. **Joe** *holds* **Tom**'s *eyes again, encouraging* **Tom** *by his serious expression to go on talking.*

Tom   Yeah, now I remember. Sure, Kitty. I wanted to be a doctor – once.

Kitty (*smiling sadly*)   I'm so glad. Because I wanted to be an actress and have a young doctor come to the theatre and see me and fall in love with me and send me flowers.

Joe *pantomimes to* **Tom**, *demanding that he go on talking.*

Tom   I would do that, Kitty.

Kitty   I wouldn't know who it was, and then one day I'd see him in the street and fall in love with him. I wouldn't know *he* was the one who was in love with me. I'd think about him all the time. I'd dream about him. I'd dream of being near him the rest of my life. I'd dream of having children that looked like him. I wouldn't be an actress all the time. Only until I found him and fell in love with him. After that we'd take a train and go to beautiful cities and see the wonderful people everywhere and give money to the poor and whenever people were sick he'd go to them and make them well again.

Tom *looks at* **Joe**, *bewildered, confused and full of sorrow.* **Kitty** *is deep in memory, almost in a trance.*

Joe (*gently*)   Talk to her, Tom. Be the wonderful young doctor she dreamed about and never found. Go ahead. Correct the errors of the world.

Tom   Joe. (*Pathetically.*) I don't know what to say.

There is a rowdy singing in the hall. A loud young **Voice** *sings, 'Sailing, sailing, over the bounding main.'*

Voice   Kitty. Oh, Kitty!

Kitty *stirs, shocked coming out of the trance.*

Voice   Where the hell are you? Oh, Kitty.

Tom *jumps up, furiously.*

Woman's voice (*in the hall*)   Who you looking for, Sailor Boy?

Voice   The most beautiful lady in the world.

Woman's voice   Don't go any further.

Voice (*with impersonal contempt*)   You? No. Not you. Kitty. You stink.

Woman's voice (*rasping, angry*)   Don't you dare talk to me that way. You pickpocket.

Voice (*still impersonal, but louder*)   Oh, I see. Want to get tough, hey? Close the door. Go hide.

Woman's voice   You pickpocket. All of you.

The door slams.

Voice (*roaring with laughter which is very sad*)   Oh – Kitty, Room 21. Where the hell is that room?

Tom (*to* **Joe**)   Joe, I'll kill him.

Kitty (*fully herself again, terribly frightened*)   Who is it?

She looks long and steadily at **Tom** *and* **Joe**. **Tom** *is standing, excited and angry.* **Joe** *is completely at ease, his expression full of pity.* **Kitty** *buries her face in the bed.*

Joe (*gently*)   Tom. Just take him away.

Voice   Here it is. Number 21. Three naturals. Heaven. My blue heaven. The west, a nest, and you. Just Molly and me. (*Tragically.*) Ah, to hell with everything.

A young **Sailor**, *a good-looking boy of no more than twenty or so, who is only drunk and lonely, comes to the bed, singing sadly.*

Sailor   Hi-ya, Kitty. (*Pause.*) Oh. Visitors. Sorry. A thousand apologies. (*To* **Kitty**.) I'll come back later.

Tom (*taking him by the shoulders, furiously*)   If you do, I'll kill you.

Joe *holds* **Tom**. **Tom** *pushes the frightened boy away.*

Joe (*sombrely*)   Tom. You stay here with Kitty. I'm going down to Union Square to hire an automobile. I'll be back in a few minutes. We'll ride out to the ocean and watch the sun go down. Then we'll ride down the Great Highway to Half Moon Bay. We'll have supper down there, and you and Kitty can dance.

Tom (*stupefied, unable to express his amazement and gratitude*)   Joe, you mean you're going to go on an errand for *me*? You mean you're not going to send me?

Joe   That's right.

He gestures toward **Kitty**, *indicating that* **Tom** *shall talk to her, protect the innocence in her which is in so much danger when* **Tom** *isn't near,* *which* **Tom** *loves so deeply.* **Joe** *leaves.* **Tom** *studies* **Kitty***, his face becoming childlike and sombre. He sets the carousel into motion, listens, watching* **Kitty***, who lifts herself slowly, looking only at* **Tom***.* **Tom** *lifts the turning carousel and moves it slowly toward* **Kitty***, as though the toy were his heart. The piano music comes up loudly and the lights go down, while* **Harry** *is heard dancing swiftly.*

Blackout.

Act Four

A little later. **Wesley**, *the coloured boy, is at the piano.* **Harry** *is on the little stage, dancing.* **Nick** *is behind the bar.* The **Arab** *is in his place.* **Kit Carson** *is asleep on his folded arms.* The **Drunkard** *comes in. Goes to the telephone for the nickel that might be in the return-chute.* **Nick** *comes to take him out. He gestures for* **Nick** *to hold on a minute. Then produces a half-dollar.* **Nick** *goes behind the bar to serve the* **Drunkard** *whisky.*

Drunkard To the old, God bless them. (*Another.*) To the new, God love them. (*Another.*) To – children and small animals, like little dogs that don't bite. (*Another. Loudly.*) To reforestation. (*Searches for money. Finds some.*) To – President Taft.

He goes out. The telephone rings.

Kit Carson (*jumping up, fighting*) Come on, *all* of you, if you're looking for trouble. I never asked for quarter and I always gave it.

Nick (*reproachfully*) Hey, Kit Carson.

Dudley (*on the phone*) Hello. Who? Nick? Yes. He's here. (*To* **Nick**.) It's for you. I think it's important.

Nick (*going to the phone*) Important! *What's* important?

Dudley He sounded like big shot.

Nick Big *what?* (*To* **Wesley** *and* **Harry**.) Hey, you. Quiet. I want to hear this important stuff.

Wesley *stops playing the piano.* **Harry** *stops dancing.* **Kit Carson** *comes close to* **Nick**.

Kit Carson If there's anything I can do, name it. I'll do it for you. I'm fifty-eight years old; been through three wars; married four times; the father of countless children whose *names* I don't even know. I've got no money. I live from hand to mouth. But if there's anything I can do, name it. I'll do it.

Nick (*patiently*) Listen, Pop. For a moment, please sit down and go back to sleep – *for me.*

Kit Carson   1 can do that, too.

He sits down, folds his arms and puts his head into them. But not for long. As **Nick** *begins to talk, he listens carefully, gets to his feet, and then begins to express in pantomime the moods of each of* **Nick**'s *remarks.*

Nick (*on phone*)   Yeah? (*Pause.*) Who? Oh, I see. (*Listens.*) Why don't you leave them alone? (*Listens.*) The church people? Well, to hell with the church people. I'm a Catholic myself. (*Listens.*) All right. I'll send them away. I'll tell them to lay low for a couple of days. Yeah, I know how it is.

Nick's *daughter* **Anna** *comes in shyly, looking at her father, and stands unnoticed by the piano.*

Nick (*on phone*)   What? (*Very angry.*) Listen. I don't like that Blick. He was here this morning, and I told him not to come back. I'll keep the girls out of here. You keep Blick out of here. (*Listens.*) I know his brother-in-law is important, but I don't want him to come down here. He looks for trouble everywhere, and he always finds it. I don't break any laws. I've got a dive in the lousiest part of town. Five years nobody's been robbed, murdered or gypped. I leave people alone. Your swanky joints uptown make trouble for you every night.

Nick *gestures to* **Wesley** — *keeps listening on the phone* — *puts his hand over the mouthpiece.*

Nick (*to* **Wesley** *and* **Harry**)   Start playing again. My ears have got a headache. Go into your dance, son.

Wesley *begins to play again,* **Harry** *begins to dance.*

Nick (*into mouthpiece*)   Yeah. I'll keep them out. Just see that Blick doesn't come around and start something. (*Pause.*) OK. (*He hangs up.*)

Kit Carson   Trouble coming?

Nick   That lousy Vice Squad again. It's that gorilla Blick.

Kit Carson   Anybody at all. You can count on me. What kind of a gorilla is this gorilla Blick?

Nick   Very dignified. Toenails on his fingers.

Anna (*to* **Kit Carson**, *with great, warm, beautiful pride, pointing at* **Nick**)   That's my father.

Kit Carson (*leaping with amazement at the beautiful voice, the wondrous face, the magnificent event*)   Well, bless your heart, child. Bless your lovely heart. I had a little daughter point me out in a crowd once.

Nick (*surprised*)   Anna. What the hell are you doing here? Get back home where you belong and help Grandma cook me some supper.

Anna *smiles at her father, understanding him, knowing that his words are words of love. She turns and goes, looking at him all the way out, as much as to say that she would cook for him the rest of her life.* **Nick** *stares at the swinging doors.* **Kit Carson** *moves toward them, two or three steps.* **Anna** *pushes open one of the doors and peeks in, to look at her father again. She waves to him. Turns and runs.* **Nick** *is very sad. He doesn't know what to do. He gets a glass and a bottle. Pours himself a drink. Swallows some. It isn't enough, so he pours more and swallows the whole drink.*

Nick (*to himself*)   My beautiful, beautiful baby. Anna, she is you again.

He brings out a handkerchief, touches his eyes and blows his nose. **Kit Carson** *moves close to* **Nick**, *watching* **Nick**'s *face.* **Nick** *looks at him.*

Nick (*loudly, almost making* **Kit Carson** *jump*)   You're broke, aren't you?

Kit Carson   Always. Always.

Nick   All right. Go into the kitchen and give Sam a hand. Eat some food and when you come back you can have a couple of beers.

Kit Carson (*studying* **Nick**)   Anything at all. I know a good man when I see one. (*He goes.*)

Elsie Mandelspiegel *comes into Nick's. She is a beautiful, dark girl, with a sorrowful, wise, dreaming face, almost on the verge of tears, and full of pity. There is an aura of dream about her. She moves softly*

and gently, as if everything around her were unreal and pathetic. **Dudley**
doesn't notice her for a moment or two. When he does finally see her, he
is so amazed he can barely move or speak. Her presence has the effect of
changing him completely. He gets up from his chair, as if in a trance, and
walks toward her, smiling sadly.

Elsie (*looking at him*)   Hello, Dudley.

Dudley (*broken-hearted*)   Elsie.

Elsie   I'm sorry. (*Explaining.*) So many people are sick. Last
night a little boy died. I love you, but –

She gestures, trying to indicate how hopeless love is. They sit down.

Dudley (*staring at her, stunned and quieted*)   Elsie. You'll never
know how glad I am to see you. Just to see you. (*Pathetically.*)
I was afraid I'd never see you again. It was driving me crazy.
I didn't want to live. Honest.

He shakes his head mournfully, with dumb and beautiful affection. Two
streetwalkers come in, and pause near **Dudley**, *at the bar.*

Dudley   I know. You told me before, but I can't help it, Elsie.
I love you.

Elsie (*quietly, sombrely, gently, with great compassion*)   I know you
love me, and I love you, but don't you see love is impossible in
this world?

Dudley   Maybe it isn't, Elsie.

Elsie   Love is for birds. They have wings to fly away on when
it's time for flying. For tigers in the jungle because they don't
know their end. We know *our* end. Every night I watch over
poor, dying men. I hear them breathing, crying, talking in their
sleep. Crying for air and water and love, for mother and field
and sunlight. *We* can never know love or greatness. We *should*
know both.

Dudley (*deeply moved by her words*)   Elsie, I love you.

Elsie   You want to live. I want to live, too, but where? Where
can we escape our poor world?

Dudley Elsie, we'll find a place.

Elsie (*smiling at him*) All right. We'll try again. We'll go together to a room in a cheap hotel, and dream that the world is beautiful, and that living is full of love and greatness. But in the morning, can we forget debts, and duties, and the cost of ridiculous things?

Dudley (*with blind faith*) Sure, we can, Elsie.

Elsie All right, Dudley. Of course. Come on. The time for the new pathetic war has come. Let's hurry before they dress you, stand you in line, hand you a gun, and have you kill and be killed.

She looks at him gently, and takes his hand. **Dudley** *embraces her shyly, as if he might hurt her. They go, as if they were a couple of young animals. There is a moment of silence. One of the streetwalkers bursts out laughing.*

Killer Nick, what the hell kind of a joint are you running?

Nick Well, it's not out of the world. It's on a street in a city, and people come and go. They bring whatever they've got with them and they say what they must say.

Sidekick It's floozies like her that raise hell with our racket.

Nick (*remembering*) Oh, yeah. Finnegan telephoned.

Killer That mouse in elephant's body?

Sidekick What the hell does *he* want?

Nick Spend your time at the movies for the next couple of days.

Killer They're all lousy. (*Mocking.*) All about love.

Nick Lousy or not lousy, for a couple of days the flatfoots are going to be romancing you, so stay out of here, and lay low.

Killer I always was a pushover for a man in uniform, with a badge, a club and a gun.

Krupp *comes into the place. The girls put down their drinks.*

Nick   OK, get going.

The girls begin to leave and meet **Krupp**.

Sidekick   We was just going.

Killer   We was formerly models at Magnin's.

They go.

Krupp (*at bar*)   The strike isn't enough, so they've got to put us on the tails of the girls, too. I don't know. I wish to God I was back in the Sunset holding the hands of the kids going home from school where I belong. I don't like trouble. Give me a beer.

Nick *gives him a beer. He drinks some.*

Krupp   Right now, McCarthy, my best friend, is with sixty strikers who want to stop the finks who are going to try to unload the *Mary Luckenbach* tonight. Why the hell McCarthy ever became a longshoreman instead of a professor of some kind is something I'll never know.

Nick   Cowboys and Indians, cops and robbers, longshoremen and finks.

Krupp   They're all guys who are trying to be happy; trying to make a living; support a family; bring up children; enjoy sleep. Go to a movie; take a drive on Sunday. They're all good guys so, out of nowhere, comes trouble. All they want is a chance to get out of debt and relax in front of a radio while Amos and Andy go through their act. What the hell do they always want to make trouble for? I been thinking everything over, Nick, and you know what I think?

Nick   No. What?

Krupp   I think we're all crazy. It came to me while I was on my way to Pier 27. All of a sudden it hit me like a ton of bricks. A thing like that never happened to me before. Here we are in this wonderful world, full of all the wonderful things – here we are – all of us, and look at us. Just look at us. We're crazy. We're nuts. We've got everything, but we always feel lousy and dissatisfied just the same.

Nick   Of course we're crazy. Even so, we've got to go on living together. (*He waves at the people in his joint.*)

Krupp   There's no hope. I don't suppose it's right for an officer of the law to feel the way I feel, but, by God, right or not right, that's how I feel. Why are we all so lousy? This is a good world. It's wonderful to get up in the morning and go out for a little walk and smell the trees and see the streets and the kids going to school and the clouds in the sky. It's wonderful just to be able to move around and whistle a song if you feel like it, or maybe try to sing one. This is a nice world. So why do they make all the trouble?

Nick   I don't know. Why?

Krupp   We're crazy, that's why. We're no good any more. All the corruption everywhere. The poor kids selling themselves. A couple of years ago they were in grammar school. Everybody trying to get a lot of money in a hurry. Everybody betting the horses. Nobody going quietly for a little walk to the ocean. Nobody taking things easy and not wanting to make some kind of a killing. Nick, I'm going to quit being a cop. Let somebody else keep law and order. The stuff I hear about at headquarters. I'm thirty-seven years old, and I still can't get used to it. The only trouble is, the wife'll raise hell.

Nick   Ah, the wife.

Krupp   She's a wonderful woman, Nick. We've got two of the swellest boys in the world. Twelve and seven years old.

The **Arab** *gets up and moves closer to listen.*

Nick   I didn't know that.

Krupp   Sure. But what'll I do? I've wanted to quit for seven years. I wanted to quit the day they began putting me through the school. I didn't quit. What'll I do if I quit? Where's money going to be coming in from?

Nick   That's one of the reasons we're all crazy. We don't know where it's going to be coming in from, except from wherever it happens to be coming in from at the time, which we don't usually like.

Krupp   Every once in a while I catch myself being mean, hating people just because they're down and out, broke and hungry, sick or drunk. And then when I'm with the stuffed shirts at headquarters, all of a sudden I'm nice to them, trying to make an impression. On who? People I don't like. And I feel disgusted. (*With finality.*) I'm going to quit. That's all. Quit. Out. I'm going to give them back the uniform and the gadgets that go with it. I don't want any part of it. This is a good world. What do they want to make all the trouble for all the time?

Arab (*quietly, gently, with great understanding*)   No foundation. All the way down the line.

Krupp   What?

Arab   No foundation. No foundation.

Krupp   I'll say there's no foundation.

Arab   All the way down the line.

Krupp (*to* **Nick**)   Is that all he ever says?

Nick   That's all he's been saying *this* week.

Krupp   What is he, anyway?

Nick   He's an Arab, or something like that.

Krupp   No, I mean what's he do for a living?

Nick (*to* **Arab**)   What do you do for a living, brother?

Arab   Work. Work all my life. All my life, work. From a small boy to old man, work. In old country, work. In new country, work. In New York. Pittsburgh. Detroit. Chicago. Imperial Valley. San Francisco. Work. No beg. Work. For what? Nothing. Three boys in old country. Twenty years, not see. Lost. Dead. Who knows? What. What-not. No foundation. All the way down the line.

Krupp   What'd he say last week?

Nick   Didn't say anything. Played the harmonica.

Arab   Old country song, I play. (*He brings a harmonica from his back pocket.*)

Krupp   Seems like a nice guy.

Nick   Nicest guy in the world.

Krupp (*bitterly*)   But crazy. Just like all the rest of us. Stark raving mad.

Wesley *and* **Harry** *long ago stopped playing and dancing. They sat at a table together and talked for a while; then began playing casino or rummy. When the* **Arab** *begins his solo on the harmonica, they stop their game to listen.*

Wesley   You hear that?

Harry   That's *something*.

Wesley   That's crying. That's crying.

Harry   I want to make people laugh.

Wesley   That's deep, deep crying. That's crying a long time ago. That's crying a thousand years ago. Some place five thousand miles away.

Harry   Do you think you can play to that?

Wesley   I want to *sing* to that, but I can't *sing*.

Harry   You try and play to that. I'll try to dance.

Wesley *goes to the piano, and after closer listening, he begins to accompany the harmonica solo.* **Harry** *goes to the little stage and after a few efforts begins to dance to the song. This keeps up quietly for some time.*

Krupp *and* **Nick** *have been silent, and deeply moved.*

Krupp (*softly*)   Well, anyhow, Nick.

Nick   Hmmm?

Krupp   What I said. Forget it.

Nick   Sure.

Krupp   It gets me down once in a while.

Nick   No harm in talking.

Krupp (*the policeman again, loudly*)   Keep the girls out of here.

Nick (*loud and friendly*)   Take it easy.

The music and dancing are now at their height.

Act Five

That evening. Foghorns are heard throughout the scene. A **Society Gentleman** *in evening clothes and a top hat, and his wife, also in evening clothes, are entering.* **Willie** *is still at the marble game.* **Nick** *is behind the bar.* **Joe** *is at his table, looking at the book of maps of the countries of Europe. The box containing the revolver and the box containing the cartridges are on the table, beside his glass. He is at peace, his hat tilted back on his head, a calm expression on his face.* **Tom** *is leaning against the bar, dreaming of love and* **Kitty**. *The* **Arab** *is gone.* **Wesley** *and* **Harry** *are gone.* **Kit Carson** *is watching the boy at the marble game.*

Lady   Oh, come on, please.

The **Society Gentleman** *follows miserably.*

The **Society Gentleman** *and* **Lady** *take a table.* **Nick** *gives them a menu.*

Outside, in the street, the Salvation Army people are playing a song. Big drum, tambourines, cornet and singing. They are singing 'The Blood of the Lamb'. The music and words come into the place faintly and comically. This is followed by an old sinner testifying. It is the **Drunkard**. *His words are not intelligible, but his message is unmistakable. He is saved. He wants to sin no more. And so on.*

Drunkard (*testifying, unmistakably drunk*)   Brothers and sisters. I was a sinner, I chewed tobacco and chased women. Oh, I sinned, brothers and sisters. And then I was saved. Saved by the Salvation Army, God forgive me.

Joe   Let's see now. Here's a city. Pribor. Czechoslovakia. Little, lovely, lonely Czechoslovakia. I wonder what kind of a place Pribor was? (*Calling.*) Pribor! *Pribor!*

Tom *leaps.*

Lady   What's the matter with him?

Man (*crossing his legs, as if he ought to go to the men's room*)   Drunk.

Tom   Who you calling, Joe?

Joe   Pribor.

Tom   Who's Pribor?

Joe   He's a Czech. And a Slav. A Czechoslovakian.

Lady   How interesting.

Man (*uncrosses legs*)   He's drunk.

Joe   Tom, Pribor's a city in Czechoslovakia.

Tom   Oh. (*Pause.*) You sure were nice to her, Joe.

Joe   Kitty Duval? She's one of the finest people in the world.

Tom   It sure was nice of you to hire an automobile and take us for a drive along the ocean front and down to Half Moon Bay.

Joe   Those three hours were the most delightful, the most sombre, and the most beautiful I have ever known.

Tom   Why, Joe?

Joe   Why? I'm a student. (*Lifting his voice.*) Tom. (*Quietly.*) I'm a student. I study all things. All. All. And when my study reveals something of beauty in a place or in a person where by all rights only ugliness or death should be revealed, then I know how full of goodness this life is. And that's a good thing to know. That's a truth I shall always seek to verify.

Lady   Are you sure he's drunk?

Man (*crossing his legs*)   He's either drunk, or just naturally crazy.

Tom   Joe?

Joe   Yeah.

Tom   You won't get sore or anything?

Joe (*impatiently*)   What is it, Tom?

Tom   Joe, where do you get all that money? You paid for the automobile. You paid for supper and the two bottles of

champagne at the Half Moon Bay Restaurant. You moved
Kitty out of the New York Hotel around the corner to the
St Francis Hotel on Powell Street. I saw you pay her rent.
I saw you give her money for new clothes. Where do you get
all that money, Joe? Three years now and I've never asked.

Joe looks at **Tom** *sorrowfully, a little irritated, not so much with* **Tom**
as with the world and himself, his own superiority; he speaks clearly,
slowly and solemnly

Joe   Now don't be a fool, Tom. Listen carefully. If anybody's
got any money – to hoard or to throw away – you can be sure
he stole it from other people. Not from rich people who can
spare it, but from poor people who can't. From their lives
and from their dreams. I'm no exception. I *earned* the money
I throw away. I stole it like everybody else does. I hurt people to
get it. Loafing around this way, I *still* earn money. The money
itself earns *more*. I *still* hurt people. I don't know who they are,
or where they are. If I did, I'd feel worse than I do. I've got a
Christian conscience in a world that's got no conscience at all.
The world's trying to get some sort of a *social* conscience, but
it's having a devil of a time trying to do *that*. I've got money.
I'll always have money, as long as this world stays the way it is.
I don't work. I don't make anything. (*He sips.*) I drink. I worked
when I was a kid. I worked *hard*. I mean hard, Tom. People are
supposed to enjoy living. I got tired. (*He lifts the gun and looks at*
it while he talks.) I decided to get even on the world. Well, you
can't enjoy living unless you work. Unless you do something. I
don't do anything. I don't *want* to do anything any more. There
isn't anything I can do that won't make me feel embarrassed.
Because I can't do simple, good things. I haven't the patience.
And I'm too smart. Money is the guiltiest thing in the world.
It stinks. Now, don't ever bother me about it again.

Tom   I didn't mean to make you feel bad, Joe.

Joe (*slowly*)   Here. Take this gun out in the street and give it
to some worthy hold-up man.

Lady   What's he saying?

Man (*uncrosses legs*)   You wanted to visit a honky-tonk. Well, *this* is a honky-tonk. (*To the world.*) Married twenty-eight years and she's still looking for adventure.

Tom   How should I know who's a hold-up man?

Joe   Take it away. Give it to somebody.

Tom (*bewildered*)   Do I *have* to *give* it to somebody?

Joe   Of course.

Tom   Can't I take it back and get some of our money?

Joe   Don't talk like a businessman. Look around and find somebody who appears to be in need of a gun and give it to him. It's a good gun, isn't it?

Tom   The man said it was, but how can I tell who needs a gun?

Joe   Tom, you've seen good people who needed guns, haven't you?

Tom   I don't remember. Joe, I might give it to the wrong kind of guy. He might do something crazy.

Joe   All right. I'll find somebody myself.

Tom *rises.*

Joe   Here's some money. Go get me this week's *Life*, *Liberty*, *Time* and six or seven packages of chewing gum.

Tom (*swiftly, in order to remember each item*)   *Life*, *Liberty*, *Time* and six or seven packages of chewing gum.

Joe   That's right.

Tom   All that chewing gum? What kind?

Joe   Any kind. Mix 'em up. All kinds.

Tom   Liquorice, too?

Joe   Liquorice, by all means.

Tom   Juicy Fruit?

Joe   Juicy Fruit.

Tom   Tutti-frutti?

Joe   Is there such a gum?

Tom   I think so.

Joe   All right. Tutti-frutti, too. Get *all* the kinds. Get as many kinds as they're selling.

Tom   *Life, Liberty, Time* and all the different kinds of gum. (*He begins to go.*)

Joe (*calling after him loudly*)   Get some jelly beans too. All the different colours.

Tom   All right, Joe.

Joe   And the longest panatella cigar you can find. Six of them.

Tom   Panatella. I got it.

Joe   Give a newskid a dollar.

Tom   OK, Joe.

Joe   Give some old man a dollar.

Tom   OK, Joe.

Joe   Give them Salvation Army people in the street a couple of dollars and ask them to sing that song that goes – (He *sings loudly.*)

Let the lower lights be burning,
Send a gleam across the wave.

Tom (*swiftly*)   'Let the lower lights be burning, send a gleam across the wave.'

Joe   That's it. (*He goes on with the song, very loudly and religiously.*)

Some poor, dying, struggling seaman,
You may rescue, you may save. (*Halts.*)

Tom   OK, Joe. I got it. *Life, Liberty, Time*, all the kinds of gum they're selling, jelly beans, six panatella cigars, a dollar for a newskid, a dollar for an old man, two dollars for the Salvation Army. (*Going.*) 'Let the lower lights be burning, send a gleam across the wave.'

Joe   That's it.

Lady   He's absolutely insane.

Man (*wearily crossing legs*)   You asked me to take you to a honky-tonk, instead of to the Mark Hopkins. You're *here* in a honky-tonk. I can't help it if he's crazy. Do you want to go back to where people *aren't* crazy?

Lady   No, not just yet.

Man   Well, all right then. Don't be telling me every minute that he's crazy.

Lady   You needn't be huffy about it.

Man *refuses to answer, uncrosses legs.*

When **Joe** *began to sing,* **Kit Carson** *turned away from the marble game and listened. While the man and woman are arguing he comes over to* **Joe**'s *table.*

Kit Carson   Presbyterian?

Joe   I attended a Presbyterian Sunday school.

Kit Carson   Fond of singing?

Joe   On occasion. Have a drink?

Kit Carson   Thanks.

Joe   Get a glass and sit down.

Kit Carson *gets a glass from* **Nick**, *returns to the table, sits down,* **Joe** *pours him a drink, they touch glasses just as the Salvation Army people begin to fulfil the request. They sip some champagne, and at the proper moment begin to sing the song together, sipping champagne, raising hell with the tune, swinging it, and so on. The* **Society Lady** *joins them, and is stopped by her husband.*

Joe   Always was fond of that song. Used to sing it at the top of my voice. Never saved a seaman in my life.

Kit Carson (*flirting with the* **Society Lady**, *who loves it*)   I
saved a seaman once. Well, he wasn't exactly a seaman. He
was a darky named Wellington. Heavy-set sort of a fellow.
Nice personality, but no friends to speak of. Not until I came
along, at any rate. In New Orleans. In the summer of the year
1899. No. '98. I was a lot younger of course, and had no
moustache, but was regarded by many people as a man of
means.

Joe   Know anything about guns?

Kit Carson (*flirting*)   All there is to know. Didn't fight the
Ojibways for nothing. Up there in the Lake Takalooca country,
in Michigan. (*Remembering*) Along about in 1881 or 2. Fought
'em right up to the shore of the Lake. Made 'em swim for
Canada. One fellow in particular, an Indian named Harry
Daisy.

Joe (*opening the box containing the revolver*)   What sort of a gun
would you say this is? Any good?

Kit Carson (*at sight of gun, leaping*)   Yep. That looks like a
pretty nice hunk of shooting iron. That's a six-shooter. Shot
a man with a six-shooter once. Got him through the palm of
his right hand. Lifted his arm to wave to a friend. Thought
it was a bird. Fellow named, I believe, Carroway. Larrimore
Carroway.

Joe   Know how to work one of these things?

He offers **Kit Carson** *the revolver, which is old and enormous.*

Kit Carson (*laughing at the absurd question*)   Know how to work
it? Hand me that little gun, son, and I'll show you all about it.

Joe *hands* **Kit Carson** *the revolver.*

Kit Carson (*importantly*)   Let's see now. This is probably a
new kind of six-shooter. After my time. Haven't nicked an
Indian in years. I believe this here place is supposed to move
out. (*He fools around and gets the barrel out for loading.*) That's it.
There it is.

Joe   Look all right?

Kit Carson   It's a good gun. You've got a good gun there, son. I'll explain it to you. You see these holes? Well, that's where you put the cartridges.

Joe (*taking some cartridges out of the box*)   Here. Show me how it's done.

Kit Carson (*a little impatiently*)   Well, son, you take 'em one by one and put 'em in the holes, like this. There's one. Two. Three. Four. Five. Six. Then you get the barrel back in place. Then cock it. Then all you got to do is aim and fire.

He points the gun at the **Lady** *and* **Gentleman** *who scream and stand up, scaring* **Kit Carson** *into paralysis. The gun is loaded, but uncocked.*

Joe   It's all set?

Kit Carson   Ready to kill.

Joe   Let me hold it.

Kit Carson *hands* **Joe** *the gun. The* **Lady** *and* **Gentleman** *watch, in terror.*

Kit Carson   Careful, now, son. Don't cock it. Many a man's lost an eye fooling with a loaded gun. Fellow I used to know named Danny Donovan lost a nose. Ruined his whole life. Hold it firm. Squeeze the trigger. Don't snap it. Spoils your aim.

Joe   Thanks. Let's see if I can unload it. (*He begins to unload it.*)

Kit Carson   Of course you can.

Joe *unloads the revolver, looks at it very closely, puts the cartridges back into the box.*

Joe (*looking at gun*)   I'm mighty grateful to you. Always wanted to see one of those things close up. Is it really a good one?

Kit Carson   It's a beaut, son.

Joe (*aims the empty gun at a bottle on the bar*)   Bang!

Willie (*at the marble game, as the machine groans*)   *Oh, boy!* (*Loudly, triumphantly.*) There you are, Nick. Thought I couldn't do it, hey? Now, watch.

The machine begins to make a special kind of noise. Lights go on and off. Some red, some green. A bell rings loudly six tunes.

One. Two. Three. Four. Five. Six.

An American flag jumps up. He comes to attention. Salutes.

Oh, boy, what a beautiful country.

A loud music-box version of the song 'America'.

Joe, **Kit Carson** *and the* **Lady** *get to their feet.*

Willie (*singing*)
My country, 'tis of thee,
Sweet land of liberty,
Of thee I sing.

Everything quietens down. The flag goes back into the machine. **Willie** *is thrilled, amazed, delighted. Everybody has watched the performance of the defeated machine from wherever he happened to be when the performance began.* **Willie**, *looking around at everybody, as if they had all been on the side of the machine.*

Willie   OK. How's that? I knew I could do it. (*To* **Nick**.) Six nickels.

Nick *hands him six nickels.* **Willie** *goes over to* **Joe** *and* **Kit Carson**.

Willie   Took me a little while, but I finally did it. It's scientific, really. With a little skill a man can make a modest living beating the marble games. Not that that's what I want to do. I just don't like the idea of anything getting the best of me. A machine or anything else. Myself, I'm the kind of a guy who makes up his mind to do something, and then goes to work and does it. There's no other way a man can be a success at anything. (*Indicating the letter 'F' on his sweater.*) See that letter? That don't stand for some little-bitty high school somewhere. That stands for me. Faroughli. Willie Faroughli. I'm an Assyrian. We've got a civilisation six or seven centuries old, I think. Somewhere along in there. Ever hear of Osman? Harold Osman? He's an Assyrian, too. He's got an orchestra down in Fresno. (*He goes to the* **Lady** *and* **Gentleman**.) I've never seen you before in my life, but I can tell from the clothes you wear and the company you keep (*graciously indicating the* **Lady**) that you're a man who looks every problem straight in the eye, and then goes to work and solves it. I'm that way myself. Well. (*He smiles beautifully, takes the* **Gentleman**'s *hand furiously.*) It's been wonderful talking to a nicer type of people for a change. Well. I'll be seeing you. So long. (*He turns, takes two steps, returns to the table. Very politely and seriously.*) Goodbye, lady. You've got a good man there. Take good care of him.

Willie *goes, saluting* **Joe** *and the world.*

Kit Carson (*to* **Joe**)   By God, for a while there I didn't think that young Assyrian was going to do it. That fellow's got something.

Tom *comes back with the magazines and other stuff.*

Joe   Get it all?

Tom   Yeah. I had a little trouble finding the jelly beans.

Joe   Let's take a look at them.

Tom   These are the jelly beans.

Joe *puts his hand into the cellophane bag and takes out a handful of the jelly beans, looks at them, smiles and tosses a couple into his mouth.*

Joe   Same as ever. Have some. (*He offers the bag to* **Kit Carson**.)

Kit Carson (*flirting*)   Thanks! I remember the first time I ever ate jelly beans. I was six, or at the most seven. Must have been in (*slowly*) eighteen – seventy – seven. Seven or eight. Baltimore.

Joe   Have some, Tom.

Tom *takes some.*

Tom   Thanks, Joe.

Joe   Let's have some of that chewing gum.

He dumps all the packages of gum out of the bag on to the table.

Kit Carson (*flirting*)   Me and a boy named Clark. Quinton Clark. Became a Senator.

Joe   Yeah. Tutti-frutti, all right. (*He opens a package and folds all five pieces into his mouth.*) Always wanted to see how many I could chew at one time. Tell you what, Tom. I'll bet I can chew more at one time than you can.

Tom (*delighted*)   All right.

They both begin to fold gum into their mouths.

Kit Carson   I'll referee. Now, one at a time. How many you got?

Joe   Six.

Kit Carson   All right. Let Tom catch up with you.

Joe (*while **Tom**'s catching up*)   Did you give a dollar to a newskid?

Tom   Yeah, sure.

Joe   What'd he say?

Tom   Thanks.

Joe   What sort of a kid was he?

Tom   Little, dark kid. I guess he's Italian.

Joe   Did he seem pleased?

Tom   Yeah.

Joe   That's good. Did you give a dollar to an old man?

Tom   Yeah.

Joe   Was he pleased?

Tom   Yeah.

Joe   Good. How many you got in your mouth?

Tom   Six.

Joe   All right. I got six, too.

Folds one more in his mouth. **Tom** *folds one too.*

Kit Carson   Seven. Seven each.

They each fold one more into their mouths, very solemnly, chewing them into the main hunk of gum.

Eight. Nine. Ten.

Joe (*delighted*)   Always wanted to do this. (*He picks up one of the magazines.*) Let's see what's going on in the world. (*He turns the pages and keeps folding gum into his mouth and chewing.*)

Kit Carson   Eleven. Twelve.

Kit Carson *continues to count while* **Joe** *and* **Tom** *continue the contest. In spite of what they are doing, each is very serious.*

Tom   Joe, what'd you want to move Kitty into the St Francis Hotel for?

Joe   She's a better woman than any of them tramp society dames that hang around that lobby.

Tom   Yeah, but do you think she'll feel at home up there?

Joe   Maybe not at first, but after a couple of days she'll be all right. A nice big room. A bed for sleeping in. Good clothes. Good food. She'll be all right, Tom.

Tom   I hope so. Don't you think she'll get lonely up there with nobody to talk to?

Joe (*looking at* **Tom** *sharply, almost with admiration, pleased but severe*) There's nobody *anywhere* for *her* to talk to – except you.

Tom (*amazed and delighted*)   Me, Joe?

Joe (*while* **Tom** *and* **Kit Carson** *listen carefully,* **Kit** *with great appreciation*)   Yes, you. By the grace of God, you're the other half of that girl. Not the angry woman that swaggers into this waterfront dive and shouts because the world has kicked her around. *Anybody* can have *her.* You belong to the little kid in Ohio who once dreamed of living. Not with her carcass, for *money,* so she can have food and clothes, and pay rent. With *all* of her. I put her in that hotel, so she can have a chance to gather herself together again. She can't do that in the New York Hotel. You saw what happens there. There's nobody anywhere for her to talk to, except you. They all make her talk like a whore. After a while, she'll *believe* them Then she won't be able to remember. She'll get lonely. Sure. People can get lonely for *misery*, even. I want her to go on being lonely for *you*, so she can come together again the way she was meant to be from the beginning. Loneliness is good for people. Right now it's the only thing for Kitty. Any more liquorice?

Tom (*dazed*)   What? Liquorice? (*Looking around busily.*) I guess we've chewed all the liquorice in. We still got Clove, Peppermint, Doublemint, Beechnut, Teaberry and Juicy Fruit.

Joe   Liquorice used to be my favourite. Don't worry about her, Tom, she'll be all right. You really want to marry her, don't you?

Tom (*nodding*)   Honest to God, Joe. (*Pathetically.*) Only, I haven't got any money.

Joe   Couldn't you be a prizefighter or something like that?

Tom   Naaah. I couldn't hit a man if I wasn't sore at him. He'd have to do something that made me hate him.

Joe   You've got to figure out something to do that you won't mind doing very much.

Tom   I wish I could, Joe.

Joe (*thinking deeply, suddenly*)   Tom, would you be embarrassed driving a truck?

Tom (*hit by a thunderbolt*)   Joe, I never thought of that. I'd like that. Travel. Highways. Little towns. Coffee and hot cakes. Beautiful valleys and mountains and streams and trees and daybreak and sunset.

Joe   There *is* poetry in it, at that.

Tom   Joe, that's just the kind of work I *should* do. Just sit there and travel, and look, and smile, and burst out laughing. Could Kitty go with me, sometimes?

Joe   I don't know. Get me the phone book. Can you drive a truck?

Tom Joe, you know I can drive a truck, or any kind of thing with a motor and wheels.

Tom *takes* **Joe** *the phone book.* **Joe** *turns the pages.*

Joe (*looking*) Here! Here it is. Tuxedo 7900. Here's a nickel. Get me that number.

Tom *goes to telephone, dials the number.*

Tom Hello.

Joe Ask for Mr Keith.

Tom (*mouth and language full of gum*) I'd like to talk to Mr Keith. (*Pause.*) Mr Keith.

Joe Take that gum out of your mouth for a minute.

Tom *removes the gum.*

Tom Mr Keith. Yeah. That's right. Hello, Mr Keith?

Joe Tell him to hold the line.

Tom Hold the line, please.

Joe Give me a hand, Tom.

Tom *helps* **Joe** *to the telephone.*

Joe (*at phone, wad of gum in fingers, delicately*) Keith? Joe. Yeah. Fine. Forget it. (*Pause.*) Have you got a place for a good driver? (*Pause.*) I don't think so. (*To* **Tom.**) You haven't got a driver's licence, have you?

Tom (*worried*) No. But I can get one, Joe.

Joe (*at phone*) No, but he can get one easy enough. To hell with the union. He'll join later. All right, call him a Vice President and say he drives for relaxation. Sure. What do you mean? Tonight? I don't know why not. San Diego? All right, let him start driving without a licence. What the hell's the difference? Yeah. Sure. Look him over. Yeah. I'll send him right over. Right. (*He hangs up.*) Thanks. (*To telephone.*)

Tom   Am I going to get the job?

Joe   He wants to take a look at you.

Tom   Do I look all right, Joe?

Joe (*looking at him carefully*)   Hold up your head. Stick out your chest. How do you feel?

Tom *does these things.*

Tom   Fine.

Joe   You *look* fine, too.

He wraps his wad of gum in Liberty *magazine.*

You win, Tom. Now, look.

He bites off the tip of a very long panatella cigar, lights it, and hands one to **Tom***, and another to* **Kit Carson***.*

Joe   Have yourself a pleasant smoke. Here.

He hands two more to **Tom***.*

Joe   Give those slummers one each. (*He indicates the* **Society Lady** *and* **Gentleman***.*)

Tom *goes over and without a word gives a cigar each to the* **Gentleman** *and the* **Lady***. The* **Gentleman** *is offended; he smells and tosses aside his cigar. The* **Lady** *looks at her cigar a moment then puts the cigar in her mouth.*

Gentleman   What do you think you're doing?

Lady   Really, dear. I'd like to.

Gentleman   Oh, this is too much.

Lady   I'd *really*, really like to, dear.

She laughs, puts the cigar in her mouth. Turns to **Kit Carson***. He spits out tip. She does the same.*

Gentleman (*loudly*)   The mother of five grown men, and she's still looking for *romance*. (*Shouts as* **Kit Carson** *lights her cigar.*) No. I forbid it.

Joe (*shouting*)   What's the matter with you? Why don't you leave her alone? What are you always pushing your women around for? (*Almost without a pause.*) Now, look, Tom.

*The **Lady** puts the lighted cigar in her mouth, and begins to smoke, feeling wonderful.*

Joe   Here's ten bucks.

Tom   Ten bucks?

Joe   He may want you to get into a truck and begin driving to San Diego tonight.

Tom   Joe, I got to tell Kitty.

Joe   I'll tell her.

Tom   Joe, take care of her.

Joe   She'll be all right. Stop worrying about her. She's at the St Francis Hotel. Now, look. Take a cab to Townsend and Fourth. You'll see the big sign. Keith Motor Transport Company. He'll be waiting for you.

Tom   OK, Joe. (*Trying hard.*) Thanks, Joe.

Joe   Don't be silly. Get going.

*Tom goes. **Lady** starts puffing on cigar. As **Tom** goes, **Wesley** and **Harry** come in together.*

Nick   Where the hell have you been? We've got to have some entertainment around here. Can't you see them fine people from uptown? (*He points at the **Society Lady** and **Gentleman**.*)

Wesley   You said to come back at ten for the second show.

Nick   Did I say that?

Wesley   Yes, sir, Mr Nick, that's exactly what you said.

Harry   Was the first show all right?

Nick   That wasn't a show. There was no one here to see it. How can it be a show when no one sees it? People are afraid to come down to the waterfront.

Harry   Yeah. We were just down to Pier 27. One of the longshoremen and a cop had a fight and the cop hit him over the head with a blackjack. We saw it happen, didn't we?

Wesley   Yes, sir, we was standing there looking when it happened.

Nick (*a little worried*)   Anything else happen?

Wesley   They was all talking.

Harry   A man in a big car came up and said there was going to be a meeting right away and they hoped to satisfy everybody and stop the strike.

Wesley   Right away. *Tonight.*

Nick   Well, it's about time. Them poor cops are liable to get nervous and – shoot somebody. (*To* **Harry**, *suddenly.*) Come back here. I want you to tend bar for a while. I'm going to take a walk over the pier.

Harry   Yes, sir.

Nick (*to the* **Society Lady** *and* **Gentleman**)   You society people made up your minds yet?

Lady   Have you champagne?

Nick (*indicating* **Joe**)   What do you think he's pouring out of that bottle, water or something?

Lady   Have you a chill bottle?

Nick   I've got a dozen of them chilled. He's been drinking champagne here all day and all night for a month now.

Lady   May we have a bottle?

Nick   It's six dollars.

Lady   I think we can manage.

Gentleman   I don't know. I *know* I don't know.

Nick *takes off his coat and helps* **Harry** *into it.* **Harry** *takes a bottle of champagne and two glasses to the* **Society Lady** *and* **Gentleman**, *dancing, collects sir dollars, and goes back behind the bar, dancing.* **Nick** *gets his coat and hat.*

Nick (*to* **Wesley**)   Rattle the keys a little, son. Rattle the keys.

Wesley   Yes, sir, Mr Nick.

Nick *is on his way out. The* **Arab** *enters.*

Nick   Hi-ya, *Mahmed.*

Arab   No foundation.

Nick   All the way down the line. (*He goes.*)

Wesley *is at the piano, playing quietly.*

The **Arab** *swallows a glass of beer, takes out his harmonica and begins to play.* **Wesley** *fits his playing to the* **Arab***'s.*

Kitty Duval*, strangely beautiful, in new clothes, comes in. She walks shyly, as if she were embarrassed by the fine clothes, as if she had no right to wear them. The* **Society Lady** *and* **Gentleman** *are very impressed.* **Harry** *looks at her with amazement.* **Joe** *is reading* Time *magazine.* **Kitty** *goes to his table.* **Joe** *looks up from the magazine, without the least amazement.*

Joe   Hello, Kitty.

Kitty   Hello, Joe.

Joe   It's nice seeing you again.

Kitty   I came in a cab.

Joe   You been crying again? (**Kitty** *can't answer. To* **Harry**.) Bring a glass.

Harry *comes over with a glass.* **Joe** *pours* **Kitty** *a drink.*

Kitty   I've got to talk to you.

Joe   Have a drink.

Kitty   I've never been in burlesque. We were just poor.

Joe   Sit down, Kitty.

Kitty (*sits down*)   I tried other things.

Joe Here's to you, Katerina Koranovsky. Here's to you. And Tom.

Kitty (*sorrowfully*) Where is Tom?

Joe He's getting a job tonight driving a truck. He'll be back in a couple of days.

Kitty (*sadly*) I told him I'd marry him.

Joe He wanted to see you and say goodbye.

Kitty He's too good for me. He's like a little boy. (*Wearily.*) I'm – Too many things have happened to me.

Joe Kitty Duval, you're one of the few truly innocent people I have ever known. He'll be back in a couple of days. Go back to the hotel and wait for him.

Kitty That's what I mean. I can't stand being alone. I'm not good. I tried very hard. I don't know what it is. I miss – (*She gestures.*)

Joe (*gently*) Do you really want to come back here, Kitty?

Kitty I don't know. I'm not sure. Everything *smells* different. I don't know how to feel, or what to think. (*Gesturing pathetically.*) I know I don't belong there. It's what I've wanted all my life, but it's too late. I try to be happy about it, but all I can do is remember everything and cry.

Joe I don't know what to tell you, Kitty. I didn't mean to hurt you.

Kitty You haven't hurt me. You're the only person who's ever been good to me. I've never known anybody like you. I'm not sure about love any more, but I know I love you, and I know I love Tom.

Joe I love you too, Kitty Duval.

Kitty He'll want babies. I know he will. I know I will, too. Of course I will. I can't – (*She shakes her head.*)

Joe Tom's a baby himself. You'll be very happy together. He wants you to ride with him in the truck. Tom's good for you. You're good for Tom.

Kitty (*like a child*)   Do you want me to go back and wait for him?

Joe   I can't tell you what to do. I think it would be a good idea, though.

Kitty   I wish I could tell you how it makes me feel to be alone. It's almost worse.

Joe   It might take a whole week, Kitty. (*He looks at her sharply, at the arrival of an idea.*) Didn't you speak of reading a book? A book of poems?

Kitty   I didn't know what I was saying.

Joe (*trying to get up*)   Of course you knew. I think you'll like poetry. Wait here a minute, Kitty. I'll go see if I can find some books.

Kitty   All right, Joe.

He walks out of the place, trying very hard not to wobble.

*Foghorn. Music. The **Newsboy** comes in. Looks for **Joe**. Is broken-hearted because **Joe** is gone.*

Newsboy (*to **Society Gentleman***)   Paper?

Gentleman (*angry*)   No.

*The **Newsboy** goes to the **Arab**.*

Newsboy   Paper, Mister?

Arab (*irritated*)   No foundation.

Newsboy   What?

Arab (*very angry*)   No foundation.

*The **Newsboy** starts out, turns, looks at the **Arab**, shakes head.*

Newsboy   No foundation? How do you figure?

Blick *and two* **Cops** *enter.*

Newsboy (*to **Blick***)   Paper, Mister?

Blick *pushes him aside. The **Newsboy** goes.*

Blick (*walking authoritatively about the place, to* **Harry**)   Where's Nick?

Harry   He went for a walk.

Blick   Who are you?

Harry   Harry.

Blick (*to the* **Arab** *and* **Wesley**)   Hey, you. Shut up.

The **Arab** *stops playing the harmonica,* **Wesley** *the piano.*

Blick (*studies* **Kitty**)   What's your name, sister?

Kitty (*looking at him*)   Kitty Duval. What's it to you?

Her voice is now like it was at the beginning of the play – tough, independent, bitter and hard.

Blick (*angry*)   Don't give me any of your gutter lip. Just answer my questions.

Kitty   You go to hell, you.

Blick (*coming over, enraged*)   Where do you live?

Kitty   The New York Hotel. Room 21.

Blick   Where do you work?

Kitty   I'm not working just now. I'm looking for work.

Blick   What kind of work?

Kitty *can't answer.*

Blick   What kind of work?

Kitty *can't answer.*

Blick (*furiously*)   WHAT KIND OF WORK?

Kit Carson *comes over.*

Kit Carson   You can't talk to a lady that way in *my* presence.

Blick *turns and stares at* **Kit Carson***. The* **Cops** *begin to move from the bar.*

Blick (*to the* **Cops**)   It's all right, boys. I'll take care of this. (*To* **Kit Carson**.) What'd you say?

Kit Carson   You got no right to hurt people. Who are you?

Blick, *without a word, takes* **Kit Carson** *to the street. Sounds of a blow and a groan.* **Blick** *returns, breathing hard.*

Blick (*to the* **Cops**)   OK, boys. You can go now. Take care of him. Put him on his feet and tell him to behave himself from now on. (*To* **Kitty** *again.*) Now answer my question. What kind of work?

Kitty (*quietly*)   I'm a whore, you son of a bitch. You know what kind of work I do. And I know what kind you do.

Gentleman (*shocked and really hurt*)   Excuse me, officer, but it seems to me that your attitude –

Blick   Shut up.

Gentleman (*quietly*)   – is making the poor child say things that are not true.

Blick   Shut up, I said.

Lady   Well. (*To the* **Gentleman**.) Are you going to stand for such insolence?

Blick (*to* **Gentleman**, *who is standing*)   Are you?

Gentleman (*taking the* **Lady**'s *arm*)   I'll get a divorce. I'll start life all over again. (*Pushing the* **Lady**.) Come on. Get the hell out of here!

The **Gentleman** *hurries his wife out of the place,* **Blick** *watching them go.*

Blick (*to* **Kitty**)   Now. Let's begin again, and see that you tell the truth. What's your name?

Kitty   Kitty Duval.

Blick   Where do you live?

Kitty   Until this evening I lived at the New York Hotel. Room 21. This evening I moved to the St Francis Hotel.

Blick   Oh. To the St Francis Hotel. Nice place. Where do you work?

Kitty   I'm looking for work.

Blick   What kind of work do you do?

Kitty   I'm an actress.

Blick   I see. What movies have I seen you in?

Kitty   I've worked in burlesque.

Blick   You're a liar.

Wesley *stands, worried and full of dumb resentment.*

Kitty (*pathetically, as at the beginning of the play*)   It's the truth.

Blick   What are you doing here?

Kitty   I came to see if I could get a job here.

Blick   Doing what?

Kitty   Singing – and – dancing.

Blick   You can't sing or dance. What are you lying for?

Kitty   I can. I sang and danced in burlesque all over the country.

Blick   You're a liar.

Kitty   I said lines, too.

Blick   So you danced in burlesque?

Kitty   Yes.

Blick   All right. Let's see what you did.

Kitty   I can't. There's no music, and I haven't got the right clothes.

Blick   There's music. (*To* **Wesley**.) Put a nickel in that phonograph.

Wesley *can't move.*

Blick   Come on. Put a nickel in that phonograph.

Wesley *does so.*

Blick (*to* **Kitty**) All right. Get upon that stage and do a hot little burlesque number.

Kitty *stands. Walks slowly to the stage, but is unable to move.* **Joe** *comes in, holding three books.*

Blick Get going, now. Let's see you dance the way you did in burlesque, all over the country.

Kitty *tries to do a burlesque dance. It is beautiful in a tragic way.*

Blick All right, start taking them off!

Kitty *removes her hat and starts to remove her jacket.* **Joe** *moves closer to the stage, amazed.*

Joe (*hurrying to* **Kitty**) Get down from there.

He takes **Kitty** *into his arms. She is crying*

Joe (*to* **Blick**) What the hell do you think you're doing!

Wesley (*like a little boy, very angry*) It's that man, Blick. He made her take off her clothes. He beat up the old man, too.

Blick *pushes* **Wesley** *off, as* **Tom** *enters.*

Blick *begins beating up* **Wesley**.

Tom What's the matter, Joe? What's happened?

Joe Is the truck out there?

Tom Yeah, but what's happened? Kitty's crying again!

Joe You driving to San Diego?

Tom Yeah, Joe. But what's he doing to that poor coloured boy?

Joe Get going. Here's some money. Everything's OK. (*To* **Kitty**.) Dress in the truck. Take these books.

Wesley's voice You can't hurt me. You'll get yours. You wait and see.

Tom Joe, he's hurting that boy. I'll kill him!

Joe (*pushing* **Tom**)   Get out of here! Get married in San Diego. I'll see you when you get back.

Tom *and* **Kitty** *go.* **Nick** *enters and stands at the lower end of the bar.* **Joe** *takes the revolver out of his pocket. Looks at it.*

Joe   I've always wanted to kill somebody, but I never knew who it should be.

He cocks the revolver, stands real straight, holds it in front of him firmly and walks to the door. He stands a moment watching **Blick**, *aims very carefully, and pulls the trigger. There is no shot.*

Nick *runs over, grabs the gun and takes* **Joe** *aside.*

Nick   What the hell do you think you're doing?

Joe (*casually, but angry*)   That dumb Tom. Buys a six-shooter that won't even shoot once.

He sits down, dead to the world.

Blick *comes out, panting for breath.*

Nick *looks at him. He speaks slowly.*

Nick   Blick! I told you to stay out of here! Now get out of here.

He takes **Blick** *by the collar, tightening his grip as he speaks, and pushing him out.*

Nick   If you come back again, I'm going to take you in that room where you've been beating up that coloured boy, and I'm going to murder you – slowly – with my hands. Beat it! (*He pushes* **Blick** *out. To* **Harry**.) Go take care of the coloured boy.

Harry *runs out.*

Willie *returns and doesn't sense that anything is changed. He puts another nickel into the machine, but he does so very violently. The consequence of this violence is that the flag comes up again.* **Willie**, *amazed, stands at attention and salutes. The flag goes down. He shakes his head.*

Willie (*thoughtfully*)   As far as I'm concerned, this is the *only* country in the world. If you ask me, *nuts* to Europe!

He is about to push the slide in again when the flag comes up again.
Furiously, to **Nick**, *while he salutes and stands at attention.*

Willie (*pleadingly*)   Hey, Nick. This machine is out of order.

Nick (*sombrely*)   Give it a whack on the side.

Willie *does so. A hell of a whack. The result is the flag comes up and*
down and **Willie** *keeps saluting.*

Willie (*saluting*)   Hey, Nick. Something's wrong.

The machine quiets down abruptly. **Willie** *very stealthily slides a new*
nickel in, and starts a new game.

From a distance two pistol shots are heard, each carefully timed.

Nick *runs out.*

The **Newsboy** *enters, crosses to* **Joe**'s *table, senses something is wrong.*

Newsboy (*softly*)   Paper, Mister?

Joe *can't hear him. The* **Newsboy** *backs away, studies* **Joe**, *wishes*
he could cheer **Joe** *up. Notices the phonograph, goes to it, and puts a coin*
in it, hoping music will make **Joe** *happier.*

The **Newsboy** *sits down. Watches* **Joe**. *The music begins. 'The*
Missouri Waltz'.

The **Drunkard** *comes in and walks around. Then sits down.* **Nick**
comes back.

Nick (*delighted*)   Joe, Blick's dead! Somebody just shot him,
and none of the cops are trying to find out who.

Joe *doesn't hear.* **Nick** *steps back, studying* **Joe**.

Nick (*shouting*)   Joe.

Joe (*looking up*)   What?

Nick   Blick's dead.

Joe   Blick? Dead? Good! That goddamn gun wouldn't go off.
I *told* Tom to get a good one.

Nick (*picking up gun and looking at it*)   Joe, you wanted to kill
that guy!

Harry *returns.* **Joe** *puts the gun in his coat pocket.*

Nick   I'm going to buy you a bottle of champagne.

Nick *goes to bar.* **Joe** *rises, takes hat from rack, puts coat on. The* **Newsboy** *jumps up, helps* **Joe** *with coat.*

Nick   What's the matter, Joe?

Joe   Nothing. Nothing.

Nick   How about the champagne?

Joe   Thanks. (*Going.*)

Nick   It's not eleven yet. Where you going, Joe?

Joe   I don't know. Nowhere.

Nick   Will I see you tomorrow?

Joe   I don't know. I don't think so.

Kit Carson *enters, walks to* **Joe**.

Joe *and* **Kit Carson** *look at one another knowingly.*

Joe   Somebody just shot a man. How are you feeling?

Kit Carson   Never felt better in my life. (*Loudly, bragging, but sombre.*) I shot a man once. In San Francisco. Shot him two times. In 1939, I think it was. In October. Fellow named Blick or Click or something like that. Couldn't stand the way he talked to ladies. Went up to my room and got my old pearl-handled revolver and waited for him on Pacific Street. Saw him walking, and let him have it, two times. Had to throw the beautiful revolver into the Bay.

Harry, **Nick**, *the* **Arab** *and the* **Drunkard** *close in around him.*

Joe *searches his pockets, brings out the revolver, puts it in* **Kit Carson**'s *hand, looks at him with great admiration and affection.* **Joe** *walks slowly to the stairs leading to the street, turns and waves.* **Kit Carson**, *and then one by one everybody else, waves, and the marble game goes into its beautiful American routine again – flag, lights and music. The play ends.*

CPSIA information can be obtained
at www.ICGtesting.com
Printed in the USA
LVHW05s1632220618
581601LV00013B/202/P

9 781408 113943